Teenagers Suck

What to do when missed curfews, texting, and "Mom, can I have the keys?" make you miserable

Joanne Kimes
and R. J. Colleary
with Rebecca Rutledge, PhD

adamsmedia
Avon, Massachusetts

dedication

To my daughter, Emily, who is soon to embark on teenhood.
Please be gentle with me. J.K.
To my former and current teens, Caitlin, Maggie, and Tess
Who taught me patience, poverty, and love.
But mostly love. B.C.

Published by
Adams Media, a division of F+W Media, Inc.
57 Littlefield Street, Avon, MA 02322. U.S.A.
www.adamsmedia.com

ISBN 10: 1-59869-898-2
ISBN 13: 978-1-59869-898-5
Printed in the United States of America.

J I H G F E D C B A

Library of Congress Cataloging-in-Publication Data
available from the publisher.

This publication is designed to provide accurate and authoritative information
with regard to the subject matter covered. It is sold with the understanding that
the publisher is not engaged in rendering legal, accounting, or other professional advice. If legal advice or other expert assistance is required, the services of
a competent professional person should be sought.
— From a *Declaration of Principles* jointly adopted by a Committee of the
American Bar Association and a Committee of Publishers and Associations

Many of the designations used by manufacturers and sellers to distinguish their
product are claimed as trademarks. Where those designations appear in this
book and Adams Media was aware of a trademark claim, the designations have
been printed with initial capital letters.

This book is available at quantity discounts for bulk purchases.
For information, please call 1-800-289-0963.

contents

acknowledgments

Acknowledgments suck. Who to thank? Exclude people, make enemies. Include people but don't say the "right" things about them, make enemies. You see where this is going. But okay. A few of these are easy, so let's start there.

My parents, Bridget and Bob Colleary. They raised my siblings and me and somehow lived to tell the tales. The fact that I have never been convicted of a felony or served a single minute in a federal correctional facility is testament to their fine work. But I do promise you that sometime between 1970 and 1977 (my teenage years) one of them turned to the other and said, "You know, dear . . . teenagers suck!"

Next stop is Joanne Kimes. This "Sucks" thing is all about Joanne (boy, that doesn't sound right, gotta make a note to change that later) and without her recommendation I would still be a non-author. She took a chance on me and hopefully isn't so disappointed that she would actually admit to it in public. Thanks, Joanne!

Now on to Meredith O'Hayre at Adams Media. She is an expert at taking the "What do I do now?" phone call and never once sent me to voicemail or put me on hold to take another call or pretended I had the wrong number. If she hadn't approved Joanne's recommendation I would still be a non-author. She also bought me lunch, which was quite tasty. Thanks Meredith!

And finally my friend Jennifer Wharton. If she hadn't introduced me to Joanne so I could be approved by Meredith I would still be a non-author. Jennifer contributed much to this book with her experiences of "TeenTown" via her long-standing mentoring work as a girls' youth soccer coach. Jennifer's help was so significant that I am donating part of my precious "Acknowledgments" space to her so she can make her own "Acknowledgments Within the Acknowledgments." I acknowledge Jennifer's acknowledging her children (and future teens), Tate Wiblin and Kelsey Wiblin. They don't suck yet.

But they will!

introduction

Like you have time to read a book. Parenting a teenager is a full-time job, because *being* a teenager is also a full-time job. Sure, they may busy themselves with school, sports, and text-messaging, but their true raison d'être is to perpetuate their teenager-ness 24/7. Which means while you are slacking off doing things like breathing and living, your teenagers are doing things like plotting and scheming. (They will throw in some sleeping as well, what with being teenagers and all.) Because their lives are all about them, and yours is all about working, cooking, cleaning, paying the taxes, and still finding time for *Dancing with the Stars*, they have the upper hand.

That's where this book comes in.

Were you ever a lifeguard? Me neither. As Woody Allen once said, I don't tan; I stroke. But as any lifeguard will tell you, the biggest threat to their personal safety is not a riptide or a shark. It's a swimmer in trouble. Yes, the very person they are dedicated to help will, in their own panic and hysteria, threaten to destroy them both. Sound familiar? That's because you're the parent of a teenager. So how do you survive? In general, there is a Plan A and there is a Plan B.

Plan A is an intricate, well thought out series of rules, chores, and boundaries designed to keep your teen in line.

Plan B is what to do when Plan A blows up in your face.

But mostly, this book is not about parenting teenagers. It's about how to survive parenting teenagers. It won't be easy, but since you're reading this it's probably too late to back out now.

It may take a whole village to raise a child, but it takes a book to raise a teenager. Because, well, *Teenagers Suck*! Before we jump right into the book, you should familiarize yourself with these:

The Ten Commandments of Parenting Teenagers

1. You are always right. And if you're not always right, it's because your parents messed you up when you were a kid.

2. Praise in public, criticize in private. Most people do the opposite. Don't be like most people.

3. Yes, you *do* have to tell them a thousand times. Stop counting and get over it. Now tell them again.

4. Your teens are smarter than you think, and stronger than you realize. So don't go acting all superior just because you have wrinkles and credit cards.

5. Remember they are growing up a lot faster than you did. Advantage, you. Growing up fast is just way overrated.

6. When they really screw up is when they need you the most. If your parents comforted you in those situations, remember how good it felt? And if they didn't, remember how much worse it made you feel?

7. Their defeats are 50 percent yours, but their victories are 100 percent theirs. Not exactly sure what that

means, it showed up in a fortune cookie. But it feels true.

8. Remind yourself, they won't be teenagers forever. Someday you will look back on these years and laugh. Definitely. Probably. Maybe.

9. Love them enough to let them hate you. Don't be their friend. Be their parent. Friends come and go. You're all-in.

10. Whatever doesn't kill you, makes you bleed internally.

(Bonus Commandment) **You can do this.**

CHAPTER I

hormones: how the simplest creatures become criminally insane

It seems like only last week your kids were playing dress-up. To look grown up, little boys drew mustaches on themselves while little girls stuffed mommy's bras. But now when you tell them to take that stuff off, you realize, they can't. They're not dressing up—they really look like that now!

One of the first and toughest adjustments about adolescence for teens and parents alike are body changes. Voices deepen. Hair sprouts. Complexions that were once peaches and cream give way to pepperoni pizza. But nothing is a tougher adjustment on some parents than watching their once-little boys and girls develop physically. And by "physically," let's cut to the chase, we're talking "sexually." Teens may become uncomfortable with their morphing bodies, but the greater challenge is for their sweating parents, because you will be freaked out big-time, and yet have to make your teen believe that you're not. So start practicing now: "Honey, you're growing up. Isn't that great? I'm so happy for you."

That was terrible. Now try it again, only convincingly this time. C'mon, it's for your kid.

Additionally, as your child becomes a different person, he is also becoming his *own* person. One who needs something that will likely jar you a bit: privacy. And although this may take some adjusting for all involved, this is not a bad thing for either of you. Because at this juncture of your teen's life, there really is a thing called TMI (Too Much Information). Giving them space, but not too much, but enough, but again not too much, is a great challenge. Think you're ready to handle it? No, actually you're not, but since you have no choice let's push on.

Taking Matters into His or Her Own Hands (AKA Masturbation)

Knock knock.
"What are you doing in there?"
Stop. Rewind. Go back.
We don't know if the birds do it or the bees do it, but teenage boys and girls definitely do it. Thanks to those raging teenage hormones, two-thirds of all teenagers admit to masturbating, and the other one-third are lying. While "sexual self-stimulation" is the PC term for this act, there

"When my flat-chested preteen told me she felt a 'bump' on her chest I panicked—cancer?! Then I thought, you can't get breast cancer until you have breasts. And that's when I realized her 'bump' meant her buds were starting to sprout."

—Alison

are many more terms for it including such classics as "whipping the two-toned trouser trout" and "auditioning the finger puppets." We'll dispense with the rest lest we end up Banned in Boston and everyplace else.

Masturbation is one of those rare things in life that is both totally normal if you do it and totally normal if you don't. It's a personal choice. In fact, what could be a *more* personal choice? During your child's toddler years, they naturally explored their bodies. Basically, your teenager is simply doing the same thing because, well, it feels good. In fact, your teen was probably masturbating before teen years.

Modern-day parents can rest assured that no one's going to go blind, become a sex fiend, or grow hairy palms as a result. They're just young human beings experimenting with their newly found physical pleasures because, well, they can. Frequency is not a concern, since some teenagers might masturbate several times a day, some once a week, but assuming that masturbation does not become your child's part-time job or after-school hobby (they can't really use it on their college applications), there's nothing to worry about. The only caveat is a nasty bit of business known as "autoerotic asphyxiation," in which boys actually choke themselves during masturbation, reducing the amount of oxygen to the brain and increasing the power of their orgasm. This dangerous practice sometimes goes awry, resulting in tragic accidental hanging deaths and much talked-about scenes in shows like *Six Feet Under*, *CSI*, and anything with Howard Stern in it. So make sure your teen knows not to try it.

No matter how open you think your relationship is with your teen, odds are this is not a topic your teenagers need or want to discuss with you. Odds are you're good with that. They may have concerns or questions, or tips for that matter, but if they need information, they will use their research skills to find answers. Your best bet is to always knock on a closed bedroom door (and wait for "come in" before opening it), don't question why it took them took so long in the bathroom, or ask why they're going through lotion at an alarming rate. If you dare to share a laugh with your teen around this topic, check out "The Contest" episode of *Seinfeld*, which is an amusing look at masturbation that never even mentions the word. Which is probably why it wasn't Banned in Boston, and everyplace else.

Pornography: The ABCs of XXX

Okay, so you're making Johnny's bed, as usual, and you're tucking in the sheets, as usual, and you bump up against something decidedly, well, unusual. Wedged in between the mattress and box spring is a DVD entitled "Hansel & Gretel & Little Red Riding Hood & Three Cans of Whipped Cream." Or something like that. You're horrified. Curious, perhaps, but horrified nonetheless. Odds are that when the doctor handed you newborn little Johnny for the first time and you gazed in wide wonder at that red little face, the thought of someday stumbling upon his porn cache was probably not what you had in mind.

Pornography is of course the most extreme form of visual sexual titillation, and it remains taboo even in a society in which it's getting pretty darned tough to find anything taboo anymore. Porn still crosses the line—and it's supposed to. But it has roots in milder, more socially acceptable "cousins" such as the Victoria's Secret catalogue, *Sports Illustrated* swimsuit issue, and pretty much every movie showing on HBO.

As we have determined (and it's even possible the more perceptive among you may have actually suspected even before picking up this book), teenage boys (and lots of teenage girls) are, at the end of the proverbial day, basically sexmad lunatics. This is what we call a "given." They can't stop, though it's not as if they're trying too hard. (Nyuk nyuk—we said "hard.") And when you combine that motivation with accessibility—the Internet delivers porn faster than Domino's delivers pizza on its best day—can Little Red Riding Hood and the Whipped Cream be far behind?

Yes, of course at this age sexual curiosity is normal, but is this a healthy way to explore that curiosity? Pornography carries with it its own politics. Backers see it as an ultimate example of both personal and sexual freedoms. Opponents often claim it's morally wrong, and specifically degrading to women.

So now what? Let's take a look at your options in this scenario.

1. Step away from the DVD. Put it back, leave it there, you never saw it.
2. Take the DVD, throw it away, and say nothing to Johnny about it.
3. Take the DVD, then later bring it to Johnny's room, shut the door, and have a little talk.

The truth is, each of these options has merit. The choice that's right for you likely depends upon your own personal belief system in areas like sex, respecting privacy, and communication. Many parents believe in acknowledging, accepting, and even honoring the separation between themselves and their children. Others see themselves and their older children as de facto contemporaries who can freely discuss anything, anywhere, anytime. Identify yourself and proceed accordingly!

Of course, none of this is meant to minimize the very real dangers associated with Internet porn which can access boy/girl, girl/girl, boy/sheep, or girl/hippo photos with only a few keystrokes. What can start off as mild curiosity can become more damaging than actually seeing Mommy and Daddy doing it. Therefore, a good parental control on your Internet browser cannot be underestimated.

Atrocious Acne

They say "Beauty is only skin-deep." Somehow "they" were never teenagers. While other unflattering physical evidence of adolescence such as bad hair, constant sleep, and growth spurts can be offset with hats, alarm clocks, and bigger clothes, hiding one's face is not so simple unless you keep moving your teen from one cold climate to another so they can wear ski masks whenever they go outside. If that's an option, bring a scarf. If it isn't, read on.

While of course not limited to teenagers, acne is thought of as an "adolescent issue" for good reason: it's estimated that 90 percent of all teens are affected. (That's even more than the 87 percent who have perfected the use of the eye-roll. But that, as they say, is another chapter.)

The best way to attack the acne issue (heck, maybe the best way to attack any issue) is to be informed. It's a popular belief that acne is caused by what kids eat or how often they wash their faces. That's right up there with the old-school popular belief that the world is flat. It's not. (Right?)

"When I was in high school my mother would ask me why I was staying home on the weekends while my friends were out having fun. I'd say, 'I'll go out as soon as my skin clears up.' That ended up being the middle of my senior year! I spent three and a half years' worth of Friday and Saturday nights hiding in my room!"

—Heather

The truth, in somewhat simplistic terms, is this: when skin cells naturally die, making room for new skin cells, they sometimes plug the hair follicles deep within the skin, trapping natural oils and bacteria inside. This blockage begins a two- to three-week process that causes pimples. And really, there ain't much you can do about it. As with many physical afflictions, acne has an element of heredity to it. So if one parent had it bad, get ready. If both parents had it bad, you might want to re-think that ski mask option.

Yes, acne is "normal," and yes, this too shall pass. One word of caution though. Because acne is difficult to hide, it can very often become the focal point of a teen's stress, also known as the Wonderful World of Drama. This can mean that they will not only become obsessed with every blemish, but that they will do anything and everything to eliminate them. This can be a bad thing. Excessive "popping" of pimples may seem like a "quick-fix" (and teens have been known to be the epitome of immediate gratification seekers), but in the long run that can lead to acne scarring, which unlike the acne itself, will not leave when adolescence does. Additionally, there are many (many) medications on the market which purport to "eliminate acne." While most are simply skin cleansers and harmless in prescribed doses, the key phrase there is "prescribed doses." Armed with a tube of gunk and a pimple, a teen's brain will deduce, "If I put on the amount it says and it'll clear up my face in seven days, then if I put on seven times the amount it says, it'll clear up my face in one day." (See: "gratification, instant.") Some cleansers can be harsh when misused, so remind your teen that abuse causes more harm than good.

When acne first strikes, it's probably a good idea to find a dermatologist and go in for a sit-down so he/she can explain Zits 101. He or she may prescribe oral antibiotics or topical creams, or, if there's a real cystic doozy that could leave a scar, may suggest an injection of a corticosteroid. Depending on how serious things get with your teen, you might want to keep the doc on speed-dial (you probably don't know how to work speed-dial, but don't worry, your teen does).

The Teen Diet: Two Pizzas and a Bowl of Cereal

Although what your teen eats may not directly affect his hormone level, his improper eating habits may give him more mood swings than a pregnant lady. Healthy bodies need healthy food for proper fueling. Teenagers do this instead:

Subject: Jeremy, 16

- Breakfast: an apple
- Snack #1: Cinnamon roll and chocolate milk
- Lunch: Tuna sandwich (eats half), chips, banana (trades it for a cookie), soda
- Snack #2: McDonald's after school. Big Mac, fries, soda

- Dinner: Chicken breast (eats half, still full from the Big Mac), pasta salad, the smallest piece of broccoli imaginable, milk
- Snack #3: Frozen pizza, soda
- Nightcap: Bowl of cereal

Subject: Melissa, 17 (self-proclaimed vegetarian)

- Breakfast: None (not hungry)
- Snack #1: Coffee and nacho chips from school vending machine
- Lunch: French fries, salad from school salad bar, diet soda
- Snack #2: Energy drink and a bagel
- Dinner: Bean and rice burrito, steamed carrots, water
- Dessert: Ice cream
- Nightcap: Popcorn (extra butter), diet soda

These typical teen diets do not exactly follow the USDA's recommended dietary guidelines. Or even common sense, for that matter. Teenagers have notoriously bad eating habits, particularly older teens who eat many of their meals outside of the family home, where school vending machines and fast-food restaurants fill them with empty calories and low nutritional value. When teenagers get busy with their friends, their sports teams, and their social lives, prioritizing smart food choices is right up there with washing behind their ears. Almost overnight, male teens seem to gain the ability to put away copious amounts of food that might rival the entire Chicago Bears defensive line. Female teens, especially those who tend to have more concern about their weight (which might be pretty much all of them), will eat less, but often make even more nutritionally unhealthy choices than their male counterparts.

"I'm on a restricted diet. Yesterday all I ate was half a cupcake, two

sodas, and a half box of cookies. I'm a sugar-tarian."

—Katie, 17

The only meals on the sample menus that are reasonably healthy and balanced are the dinners these two teenagers eat with their families at home. Coincidence? Not. One of the best ways to assist your teenager in eating better is to make it a priority to eat at least one sit-down family meal per day. That's right, lock 'em down and fill 'em up. Shackle them to the table if needed. And try to minimize the junk when you go grocery shopping. If you don't put it in the house, they can't eat it. Unless they get it from somewhere else. Which they will. But don't think about that, you'll only get depressed.

Another problem for teens is skipping breakfast, which we know is just plain wrong. This is often created by the fact that they are always sleep-deprived and refuse to get out of bed until the last possible minute. See if you can find out what they'll eat in the morning, even if it's not traditional "breakfast food." A burger? Why not, you'd let them eat it for lunch and it's no tougher to make than eggs. Pizza? Has all the basic food groups, and you know they'll eat it. Chocolate cake? Okay, too far; avoid refined sugar like the plague at breakfast since it'll give them just enough energy to get them to school where they will crash and burn and flunk out and end up living with you forever. If you can't get your teen to simultaneously sit and eat, try buying some on-the-go type breakfast foods (as low in sugar as possible) that they can easily grab and eat, well, on-the-go. Ask your teenager for some suggestions about what they would be willing to eat on the run. They'll like being included and your parental guilt will be minimized. Hey, take your victories where you can get them.

Ultimately, this "food fight" may appear to be totally unwinnable. And it sort of is. But don't give up, because you are still teaching and modeling good nutritional options for your teenagers by the way you shop and eat. While it may seem like they don't care and aren't watching . . . well, they probably aren't. But in case they are, just stay on the safe side and do the right thing.

Waking Up at the Crack of Noon

It's a typical Saturday. Breakfast is a distant memory, lunch has come and gone, and your teenager still hasn't crawled out from her lair; still snoozing away behind closed doors, snuggled happily under the covers or maybe even hanging upside down from the ceiling, who knows. Waking them is a great idea, if you have masochistic tendencies. Ah, those moans and groans sure to emanate from your precious vampire, who will be grumpy and monosyllabic until darkness falls, when they will become the life of the party as everyone else clamors for a decent night's rest. Garlic and crosses won't protect you here, so you'll need a plan.

Why does every teen's body clock take on this dramatic "turning day into night and night into day" shift? Contrary to popular belief, this sudden change in sleep habits does not mean your teen has become lazy, unmotivated, and antisocial. Most likely, your teen was already lazy, unmotivated, and antisocial! No, those pesky teen hormones are to blame here, as normal waking/sleeping cycles seem to swap places like those pesky twin girls did in *The Parent Trap*. These erratic sleeping patterns can disrupt the household and drive parents crazy, but unfortunately, research has shown that this time clock shift is biological. During Those Zany Vampire Years, standard time (which our world lives by) doesn't mesh very well with teen time (which their world lives by). As frustrating as that may be, it is normal for your teenager to feel sleepy during the daytime and then be wired at night. Yes it's a pain in the neck, but that's what vampires do, so get used to it.

What You Can Do about Elvira
Dig deep for some extra understanding of the great sleep-till-noon syndrome, but also insist on some basic ground rules that will keep it from splattering onto the rest of the family. Go knock on her casket and explain that on weekends you're flexible, but that when the household goes to bed, the teen must stay quietly in her lair with no audible noise. On school nights, set a hard-and-fast bedtime. Teenagers, even the vampiric kind, need eight to nine hours of sleep per night. Most won't get it, but do your best to enforce it. While you can't force a vampire to sleep (face it, it's not easy to force a vampire to do much of anything), you do have the power to make it seem like a good alternative. A realistic cut-off time for TV, Internet, loud music, and telephone use is a start. Without those, what is there to stay awake for? If needed, swipe their computer keyboards and cell phones and keep them in your room for overnight "safekeeping" (wink wink). Hey, it beats your other option, which of course is to drive a stake through the vampire's heart. Which really makes no sense, because who then would clean the garage?

Boys will be boys. This we know. But what does it mean? In this case, it's actually good news! When adolescence hits boys, their brand of crazy tends to become internalized. Yes, they are legally insane at this point, but at least they are considerate enough to keep it mostly to themselves. (Unlike their sisters, who make the whole family—if not world—suffer.) Perhaps the most significant change for a boy reaching puberty is that he automatically begins a new relationship—with his penis.

A Boner-Fide Problem

Erections are hard. Hmmm, no, bad, let's start over.
Erections are a big problem. Not even close.
Erections are a funny thing. Yes. Let's go with that.
Some boys start having erections young, very young, way young, sometimes even before they're born. (Now that's young.) These pre-pubescent erections of course have no sexual foundation and are purely physical, totally normal, and just plain amusing. Although—disclaimer—laughing and pointing at your toddler's erect little penis is not recommended and may cause subconscious issues which could result in massive shrink bills in later years. And remember, eventually they will be the ones deciding where you'll spend your twilight years. You've been warned.

Technically speaking, erections are caused when a pair of tubes running the length of the penis, the corpora cavernosa, become engorged with venous blood. Does that bring sexy back or what? Maybe not, but that's okay. Many erections have nothing to do with sexual impulse at all and are the result of various stimuli that could be explained here, but frankly science isn't my strong suit so let's move on.

When boys hit puberty, generally twelvish but that can vary, hormones start to fly and so do the erections. More and more often as the concept of the birds and the bees and cheerleaders become introduced. Statistics show teenage boys' thoughts are broken down thusly, as illustrated in this pie chart:

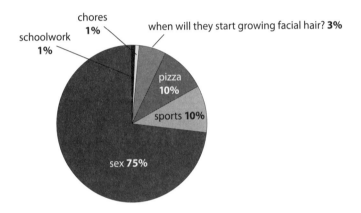

Okay, that's not really true. But who knows, it might be. Suffice it to say that your adolescent son has sex on the brain. And on other body parts as well. Remember this: every teenage boy is an erection waiting to happen.

Erections have many aliases, including but not limited to hard-on, boner, rod, chubby, stiffy, fatty, woody, and pocket rocket. Americans don't have a patent on slang, either. The Cantonese call it *chia kei*, which means "rising flag." In Spanish, it's *levantamiento en la región sur*, or "uprising in the southern region." And leave it to the Dutch to come up with *Ontzettend Dikke Ochtend Lul*, or **ODOL** for short, which is translated literally as "really fat morning cock." Ah, those smooth-talking Dutch. But odds are your teenage boy has other names for it. Why don't you ask him? Kidding!

That actually brings us to the nicest part about this topic. Although this book is largely about how to better communicate with your teen, the truth is some topics fall under the "TMI" (Too Much Information) banner, and this is one of them. There really is no good reason why, as a matter of course, you should ever discuss erections with your teenager.

Your biggest challenge here is to avoid going into denial about your teenage boy's erections. They are the precursor to his becoming a sexual being, and many parents have a very difficult time even thinking of that, much less accepting it. Just keep in mind that the last thing he wants to do is think about you having sex, too. So you're even.

**The Three Most Common Reasons
Teenage Boys Get Erections:**
1. A dog somewhere is barking.
2. An airplane is flying overhead.
3. It's Thursday.

**The Three Most Common Places
Erections Will Occur:**
1. High school hallways
2. While watching *The Girls Next Door* marathon on the E! Channel
3. Church

Some Dry Humor about Wet Dreams

If you're the parent of a teenage son, you may very well find yourself faced with some challenges regarding their sheets. As in seeing them wadded up in a corner of his closet, or finding them "missing" in the neighbor's trash can. That's because between the ages of twelve and fourteen many boys begin to have "wet dreams" (nocturnal emissions). These occur when boys ejaculate while sleeping. You might want to consider discussing "wet dreams" with your son before one occurs, since having him wake up the morning after might be just a touch freaky if he has no idea what just happened. A boy with semen-stained pajama bottoms is not going to be a happy camper over his bowl of Cheerios.

Wet dreams are totally normal and tend to occur as a release from the buildup of hormones in the early teen years. They can be caused by sexual excitement while dreaming or by stimulation from rubbing against blankets or pillows. Research indicates that the two biggest concerns for teen boys about wet dreams are that having these dreams and ejaculations are a sign of sexual abnormalities or deviant thoughts, and/or that having wet dreams means you are gay. If you are able to have a pre-emptive discussion with your son, assure him that wet dreams are not abnormal or deviant and they have nothing to do with determining sexual orientation.

While these wet dreams are absolutely a normal, natural occurrence for boys during puberty and their growing sexual development, wet dreams are often worrisome and embarrassing to both boys and the parents who wash the sheets. When and if wet dreams happen to your teenager, please try to be understanding and remember that your son is already feeling embarrassed and should not be made to feel shame or guilt. Additionally, wet dreams are subconscious and cannot be avoided or controlled. Remember that moments like this will be uncomfortable for both parent and son. The best thing you can do to help your son is to reassure him that what's happening with his body is normal and then teach him how to run the washing machine and make his own bed.

The good news is that the frequency of wet dreams is often diminished as your youngster starts to mature and begins to express his sexual self through masturbation and eventually by becoming sexually active. Still waiting for the good news, huh?

Going with the Flow—Managing Menstruation

Sugar and spice and everything nice, that's what little girls are made of. But when those little girls enter their tumultuous teens, you'll need to toss in a few more ingredients. That's because when the hormones hit that changes them from "girl" to "woman," you'll need a few items from drugstore shelves and lingerie departments.

When Tony, a divorced father of two daughters, discovered four pairs of balled-up bloodied underpants in the closet after a weekend visit with his girls, he was dismayed. Did thirteen-year-old Lacey have her period already? Why hadn't she told him? What was he supposed to say or do now that he has the blood-stained evidence in hand? Tony is a devoted father who adores his daughters and yet he finds himself totally perplexed by this situation.

As our young teenage girls enter puberty, generally sometime between the ages of eleven and fourteen, they will most likely have their first menstruation/period. Preparation is key here—can you imagine how frightening it would be for a girl who has no clue what's happening to her body to see blood in her underpants? We all know blood belongs on the inside! Therefore, it's important to ensure that your teenage girl knows the ins and outs of menstruation. Many girls will have already had conversations with their friends and will be virtual encyclopedias of information, as well as misinformation. Some preteens will have had a sex education class in school and know what to expect, while others will need a sit-down with mom (or a very brave dad) to better understand what will happen to their bodies during menstruation. Others will do better having a book on the topic casually dropped on their bed, never ever to be mentioned again. Hint: try *The Care & Keeping of You: The Body Book for Girls* (American Girl Library) by Valorie Lee Schaefer.

All teenage girls will be emotional about this event to some extent. Some may view getting their first period as a momentous occasion fit for celebration (really, can "Period Parties" and Hallmark cards be far off?), while others will be horrified for anyone else to know ("Please don't tell DAD!"). It makes sense to talk to your daughter ahead of time to find out which camp she falls into. Regale her with your most embarrassing period story and make it seem funny, no matter how it nearly ruined your life. She doesn't have to know that part.

Things with Wings, and Other Must-Haves to Go with the Flow

Of course, she'll need gear. You can travel the sanitary pad or tampon route. While tampons are becoming increasingly popular, it may be best for young teens to start with pads because they are easier to manage until girls become more regular in their menstrual cycle, which can be as short as a few months or as long as a year. If you want to offer assistance or your daughter seeks your help in learning to insert a tampon, have her read the directions and look at the diagram on the box. Then, if she is willing to allow you to help her, use a hand mirror to show her the different entry points into her vagina so she won't be trying to insert it up her urethra (like you did when you were a kid because you only had the crummy attached pencil sketch as a guide). Then, touch the small of her back so she knows where to aim. This is also commonly known as "mother-daughter bonding."

Be sure to warn her about the dangers of toxic shock syndrome and the importance of changing tampons every four to eight hours. Then, prepare yourself for tears and frustration and insane ranting. From you as well as her. Because any embarrassment and/or discomfort will definitely be "All your fault!" But hey, you knew that.

More good news! Along with the joys of blood flow, your teenager will now be joining The Wonderful World of PMS. Hmm, crying jags, moodiness, and unpredictable behavior . . . how will you ever be able to tell whether she has PMS or she's just being a teenager? Do your best to assuage these issues with lots of sympathy, a heating pad, a good over-the-counter pain reliever, some Omega-3 fish oil capsules (for her), and a spa day (for you).

As for poor, perplexed Tony, his best bet would be to wash the underwear (a good pre-treater makes all the difference), buy some pads and a few other unrelated drugstore goodies like shampoo, conditioner, and body wash, and leave them in his daughter's room. When she asks about them, he should tell her he picked up some things he thought she might need and if she wants to talk about any of them, he knows a lot about shampoo and conditioner. Tony's daughter will get the message that he knows and cares, but will appreciate not needing to have a discussion. Another reminder that sometimes the best communication is nonverbal.

Another possibility would be to have a trusted female relative or friend talk to Tony's daughter about the changes going on with her body. The ultimate goal is for your teen to feel comfortable and informed.

Bras: Lifting and Separating Fact from Fiction

Somewhere along the line, the fundamental evolution of human development got all mixed up with marketing and societal overthink and the next thing you know simple things become complicated. Case in point: the bra. Somehow, bras are now an indication of sexual maturity, thus setting off what the Temptations would call a "Ball of Confusion." Who looks at thirteen-year-old girls and thinks, "You're a woman now"? Other than thirteen-year-old boys, that is. Come on now, people, it's just underwear!

Back in the proverbial day, bras were being burned and the Marlo Thomas epic, "Free to Be You and Me" had more than one meaning. In the mainstream media, feminism roared and bras were often thought of as a bad thing—binding, constricting, and downright unpleasant. They were seen as a tool to keep women in their place. So to speak.

Forty years later, while a bra still does not a woman make, preteen and teenage girls today see them in a whole different light. Girls as young as eight and nine years old are asking to wear a bra. While some girls actually need them very early on, many girls are just doing it for the grown-up factor. Thirteen-year-olds want leopard print push-up bras from sexy lingerie shops. Thanks to the media's apparent preoccupation with encouraging every kid to grow up too fast, teenage girls wearing bras feel powerful, sexy, and adult.

"When I got my first bra, it was so uncomfortable. It dug into me and the straps kept falling down. My mom said I'd get used to it; but between my braces and headgear, I had enough things to get used to already."
—Bailey, 11

This much we know: somewhere between the ages of nine and fifteen, girls develop breasts. While this is a natural part of puberty, it does impact some girls differently than others. Some girls are pleased and proud to have their bodies changing and other girls may feel shy and frightened.

At age thirteen, Kelly began wearing her bathing suit under her clothes every day to hide her developing breasts, because she hated them and was not sure how to handle her body's changes. At age twelve, Samantha, who had no breast buds at all, insisted to her mother that she needed a bra. Not a "sports bra"—a real bra—which to her meant lacy, red, and padded!

Somewhere between these two extremes lies the truth for your daughter. How you approach the bra issue will have a great deal to do with your own values and morals and your daughter's age when the time comes to bra shop. It can be an emotional issue for some teens and for others it's just a day at the mall. Some girls will love to participate in the process. They'll make a special day of it with mom while some girls will moan and groan when you bring home the plainest white sports bra top. While you can certainly guess where on the spectrum your daughter will fall, you may not know ahead of time which kind of girl yours will turn out to be. Proceed delicately. Open a dialogue and remember that discussing the need and then finding a bra for you daughter is going to be a bit of a trial and error process. Selection, sizing, and appropriateness for her body and her age are going to be issues.

Most importantly, be tactful and sensitive. Understand that in today's society bras are not just underwear—teens view them as a way to make a statement. You need to ascertain what your daughter's statement is going to be and discuss it with her. If you have a preteen or younger teen, do a little research beforehand. Look around your daughter's social circle and talk to other mothers. Are most girls her age wearing bras? Is it because they need them or is it a peer pressure/fashion issue? Armed with this information, choose a time, perhaps on an unrelated shopping trip, to casually ask your daughter what she thinks about bras and take your cues from her about what her wants and needs may be. Do your best to give your daughter guidance and emotional support and talk to her early and often about her changing body. If you feel comfortable talking—eventually—she will too.

Perhaps sharing a story about your own early experience with bras may help make your daughter feel more at ease if she seems anxious about the process. Try to see this as an early opportunity to connect with your daughter and set some groundwork for some of the more difficult conversations still ahead.

CHAPTER 2

mars, venus, & teentown

Unless you live under a rock, or in one of those states with more rocks than people, by now you're familiar with the philosophy that the book *Men Are from Mars and Women Are from Venus* made famous. The theory is that the xx and xy are from different emotional planets and think different thoughts, feel different feelings, follow different rules, and speak different languages. But with all due apologies to John Gray, while he may believe that Men + Women = Everyone, he overlooked the fact that the universe is inhabited by a third group: Teenagers.

While this mysterious race does have certain human-like qualities, there's something vaguely podlike about them. They have ears, yet cannot hear when you ask them to take out the garbage. They have eyes, yet cannot see that their rooms look like they've been vandalized. They have mouths, yet cannot speak the words "Please" or "Thank you" or "No, you sit, I'll do it." For our purposes, let's not hand them over an entire planet—they'd only litter it with wet towels on the floor and leftover fast-food containers under their beds. But let's at least give them their own locale: TeenTown.

Things are different in TeenTown than they are on Earth. TeenTown has its own laws, style of dress, musical taste, and their own ideas about right (always them) and wrong (usually you). And while it's true that TeenTown exists only inside the heads of adolescents, the sooner you realize it's all real to them, the better. They have their own code. Your mission, should you decide to accept it, is to decode it without driving yourself permanently crazy. To help you understand what you're up against, enjoy this snappy little tune:

The TeenTown National Anthem
O say, can you see
By the dawn's early light
House party ran real late
And now home I am sneaking

So I head for my room
If they catch me it's doom
Can't wake up Mom and Dad
If I do they'll be freaking

They'd confiscate my phone
With the custom ring tone

Take back their credit card
Make me work in the yard

O say, does that sound like
It would be any fun?

Like no, it would so suck
Can't wait to be twenty-one!

The Human ATM

This sound familiar? You're whipping money out of your wallet to hand your teen so often that you've given yourself carpal tunnel syndrome? Or maybe you're thinking about getting a weekend job just to afford your teenager? Or you've actually made the phone call (disguising your voice of course) to inquire how much the Red Cross is paying these days for a pint of blood?

Money may or may not be the root of all evil, but it sure can be the root of a lot of parent-teen conflict. When children are, well, children, they generally don't cost much. A Happy Meal here, a coloring book there, some hand-me-downs from an older sibling or sympathetic friend, and it's all good. Well, hopefully you enjoyed the good old days, because they're so over and they're not coming back. While you're struggling to accept that, here's how to deal with it.

You have three issues to face here:

1. Teenagers want things.
2. Teenagers need things.
3. Teenagers expect you to give them the things they want, plus the things they need.

We have all heard the adage that teenagers will "eat you out of house and home." But if you're not careful, they might "clothes you" out of house and home and "technology you" out of house and home as well.

"When they were babies, my kids called me 'DaDa.'

When they got older, they called me 'Daddy.' Now that they're

teenagers, they call me 'Hi, Can I Have Twenty Dollars?'

—Doug, father of four teenagers

First off, realize that teenagers are expensive to maintain. (Think of them as yachts with messy rooms.) Secondly, make sure they realize it too. The more you can steer your teens toward Appreciation and away from Entitlement, the better your chances of maintaining some non-gray hairs. This is where you dust off your "When I was your age, my allowance was a nickel and I wasn't allowed to spend it all in one place!" stories. You know you have them. And if you don't, use the ones your parents told you.

But be prepared for resistance. Your teen remembers childhood too, a time when you met all their needs and probably most of their wants, as well. But now that Happy Meal has evolved into sushi, and that coloring book is now an iPhone, and those hand-me-downs have given way to designer labels. As far as they're concerned, nothing has really changed. You're still financing this expedition, right? Right? Right?

Let Them Make Their Own Financial Mistakes

The truth is, money matters create a situation ripe for long-term, big-picture growth. You taught them how to make a bed, you taught them how to ride a bike, and now you need to teach them about money. But beware: the words "supply-side economics" won't even be out of your mouth before your offspring will utter The Teen Mantra: "Can I have that?"

**Here's a Mom-Teen Exchange Overheard
Recently at the Local Mall**

Teen: I love these boots, if I don't get them I'll just die!
Mom: Fine, you can buy them with your own money.
Teen: Oh well then never mind.

In order to instill any financial knowledge (or, as your Dad told you, "The value of a dollar"), it's vital to let teenagers spend their own money. Realize this means they will spend it very, *very* badly. When they do, do your best Marcel Marceau imitation and say nothing. (But don't try that "walking against the wind" thing all mimes do because that's a hard one to pull off.) Give them time to learn the value of saving. They will, especially when they find something they really really *really* want, which will happen at exactly the same time they are really really *really* broke. Don't give them the money. Let them learn the lesson.

So What to Do?

At the end of the proverbial day, it all comes down to this: what are you willing to pay for, and what are you not? While these are individual choices based upon individual circumstances, and no two families will handle this situation the same way, the only non-negotiable point is to make your rules and stick to them.

It's probably prudent to supply all of the necessities, and some of the luxuries. But reserve the right to define the terms here, since teenagers' "necessity vs. luxury" lists will often (as in *always*) differ from your own, and will probably have you scratching your head and believing they must get this questionable thought process genetically from their other parent, because you have way too much sense for them to have gotten it from you.

So now that we've established that teenagers will have financial needs, as well as wants (some less unreasonable than others), the bottom line becomes "Where does this money come from?"

When it comes to teenagers earning spending money outside the home, there are two camps. Some families not only allow but encourage their teenagers to find part-time work after school and on weekends as early as they're able. Other families believe that work will come soon enough in life, and want their teens to concentrate more on school and just being young, footloose, and fancy-free while they still can. Just remember, if their fancy is free, that means someone else is footing the bill for it, and that someone is y-o-u.

There are also differing philosophies within the home. Some families assign regular, steady chores and create allowances. Other families are open to their teenagers doing extra jobs around the house for cash. So when one hears the magic words—in TeenSpeak, those are "I need money"—your Pavlovian response should be "And I need my car washed." Or "And I need the garage cleaned." But never "So go rob a bank," because with your luck this is the time they would actually listen to you. (For more information on chores, see "Chores & Responsibilities" in Chapter 5.)

Keep in mind that a recurring theme to your survival of their adolescence is "separation." A good start would be for your teen to maintain her own bank account. (But don't put their college money in there! Or even *think* about giving them their own credit card!) If you create a consistent, well-communicated system, you should be able to avoid becoming The Human ATM.

In Teen We Trust . . . NOT!

Recently a group of high school students was asked the question, "Should parents in general trust their teenagers?" Their answer was instantaneous. "No way," they replied. They were then asked, "Should your parents trust you?" Again, immediate answer. "Yes," they said. The game is afoot.

Let's start off with The Trust Quiz. Let's make it as easy as humanly possible. Pass/Fail. One question.

True or False: "I trust my teenager."

If you answered "True," you failed. Totally, completely, and miserably failed. Don't worry, it's not going on your permanent record.

It was a trick question, of course, but keep in mind that with teenagers *all* questions are potentially trick questions. They will hear the words they want to hear and reply in ways that can be defended later as "misunderstandings." Remember that teens, AKA manipulation machines, are of course following the laws of TeenTown. One of the biggies there (perhaps only below "Up All Night, Sleep All Day" and "Pizza 24/7") is, "Do what's best for you and don't let your parents stop you since they don't understand." This is why the adorable apple of your eye who in fact played Apple #3 (the best of the apples by far) in the first-grade play can stand in front of you today as a teenager, smile that same smile (albeit with more teeth), and lie right to your face.

> "I work hard to keep my parents' trust.
>
> That's how I get away with things."
>
> —Nikki, 18

Let's be clear: some teenagers *are* trustworthy. (Right up until they're not.) And these are the most dangerous of all, because we tend to forget that they are still teenagers, and their lack of experience and a fully formed brain means they are prone to lapses of all types. Don't let your guard down. Remember this: it is not your job as a parent to trust your teenager. It is your job as a parent to make sure your teenager is trustworthy.

Christi, now raising her third (and final) teenager, offers this thought: "I always trust my daughter, but rarely her judgment." This is an important distinction. Let's analyze exactly what it means.

First, the "I always trust my daughter" part. In Christi's case, she's saying she trusts her daughter to be honest with her. Yes, shocking as it may seem, teenagers have been known to stretch the truth a little, and even (gasp) outright lie. Why? Well, teenagers lie for the same two basic reasons children (and even adults) lie: either to get something they want, or to avoid getting into trouble. Hope and pray that your teens are bad liars. That will make things simpler all the way around and better for them, and you, in the long run. Your best bet is to make your teens accountable. This is not punishment, it's parenting. (Well, sometimes the two overlap/mingle, like a vanilla/chocolate swirl soft-serve ice cream cone.) And don't be swayed by the classic TeenSpeak plea "Don't you trust me?" Don't let them throw it back on you—you'll be the one to ask the questions around here!

Now to the second half of Christi's philosophy: she always trusts her daughter ". . . but rarely her judgment." This situation is a bit more complicated because it involves your teen out in the world with other teens who may be even less responsible than yours. Say your teen isn't driving yet, or doesn't have car access, and is going out with friends. When you're told "I'll get a ride home," can your teen make a good decision about avoiding the "crazy" driver in the group, or maybe one that has consumed alcohol or drugs? Just because your teen has parents committed to ensuring their kid is safe doesn't mean their friends do. Sure, your teen's friends *seem* nice and smart and trustworthy. Two words for you: Eddie Haskell. As a result, Christi is a very "hands-on" Mom. She hosts the parties, she does the driving, and she knows where her daughter is at all times and with whom. Does Christi's daughter feel stifled? "Sometimes," she confides. "But it also tells me 'My mom cares about me.'" Bingo. Be brave enough to be the tough parent when tough is called for. Lenient/checked-out parents are a dime a dozen. Even cheaper when there's a sale on.

Christi's daughter aside, don't believe your teen until your teen has proved him/herself believable. Remember, you can love them without trusting them. It's okay. When they claim their homework is done, take a look at it. When they say their room is clean, inspect it. When they're out at night, be there (and awake) to be sure they make curfew. It's behavior modification, and once they know what is expected of them, and that you're watching them like a hawk, they'll start to do it on their own. And if they don't, well, that's why God created grounding.

"Home, James"—Your Life as the Chauffeur

Feel free to skip this section if you actually have a chauffeur. Of course, if you do, your teens are probably being raised by a team of nannies anyway, so just go ahead and give them this book on your way out the gates to play polo with your pals Buffy and Biff. But, for those of you still here . . .

Cars don't drive themselves. At least not yet. So until they do, someone needs to be behind the wheel. Eventually, that someone will be your teenager. (Breathe. It'll be okay. Promise. Just breathe.) We'll get to that momentous life-changing super-stressor in another chapter, but for now let's talk about how to survive when the person behind the wheel is not your predriving teen, but you.

When kids are little, they do what you want. Eventually, when they are on their own, they will do what they want. (Keep breathing.) But this is that gawky in-between phase, where you are actually doing what THEY want. It's thankless, grueling, and never-ending. Making it, of course, a perfect microcosm for parenthood. Enjoy.

Some parents believe a busy teen is a happy teen. Others think of it as idle hands being the devil's workshop. Neither perspective is wrong. The difference may be as simple as whether you live in a blue state or a red state. The bottom line is that teenagers will have activities, whether school-related, sports-related, church-related, or so on. Regardless of what they're into, it's good for them to do something besides eat, sleep, watch TV, torment their siblings, surf the Internet, and drop wet towels on the floor.

And while participating in outside-the-home activities is good for their budding independence, there is an irony strongly at work here: you have to help them become independent. The good news is, they have places to go and people to see. The bad news is, they can't drive yet. Of course the other good news is . . . they can't drive yet.

It goes without saying that circumstances will differ based upon where you might live, what your mass transit options are, whether your kids consider bicycles to be transportation or punishment, and whether they are willing to put one foot in front of the other and actually walk to places other than the refrigerator. But ultimately if you have pre-driving teens, at least to some degree you will be called to serve. Think of it as jury duty that just goes on and on and on. And on.

But.

You know how we tend to focus on bad cholesterol, forgetting in the process that there's good cholesterol too? There actually is some upside to being the chauffeur. Being in the car with them, to and from, affords you the chance to find out more about what makes them tick. You can also find out what they're looking forward to (when en route) and what they experienced (while coming back). Take advantage of this time. Since other parents will be undoubtedly shirking their duties, you will also find yourself transporting their kids from time to time. When that happens, pretend you're listening to your classic rock station on the car stereo and eavesdrop. Their backseat conversations will give you a little better idea of which of them your teens should be hanging out with . . . or staying away from. And of course by transporting your kids yourself you know they'll get where they need to go safe and sound. Nothing wrong with that.

And that's it. If you expected this section to talk about how to avoid being your kids' chauffeur . . . sorry. Death, taxes, driving your kids around. Unavoidable. So relax, things could be worse. And soon, when your teen starts driving, they will be!

Picking Your Battles #1: When to Make Peace

Fight or flight. We all have it, we all use it. Get ready to use it like you have never used it before.

Ever see a toddler in the throes of some tantrum and think to yourself, "Whew, glad those days are over. There's no negotiating with terrorists"? That little mantra can help you keep your wits about you with madness in your midst, whether it's five-year-old madness or fifteen-year-old madness. First off, don't panic. You never hear "They panicked and everything worked out fine." You only hear "They panicked and now everybody's dead." So just relax and remember that whenever a potential battle presents itself, you can either let it go, or wage war.

Just remember you've been doing this sort of refereeing/problem solving for years. Just recall the days when your toddler wanted to wear pajamas to school . . . when your seven-year-old refused to eat anything other than popcorn . . . when you saw your ten-year-old skateboarding without a helmet even though you had just put it on him yourself? You survived those skirmishes and you will survive these battles, too. The stakes may feel a bit higher in the teen years, but these new dramas are not really so different from the ones that have come before. And will no doubt come later as well.

Your teenage son stuns the family by coming out of his room one morning with a new look. It includes blue hair and black lipstick. He saunters to the breakfast table and dares anyone to comment.

You will want to scream, "What has happened to my sweet little boy with his curls and dimpled chin?" But do yourself a favor: scream on the inside. His sister says, "Can I borrow your lipstick?" They burst out laughing. Wait! Your boy is still in there somewhere . . . under the blue hair. This sudden appearance change may be disturbing, unattractive, and annoying, but before you react, think to yourself, "This is not life-threatening." This is one to let go.

Perhaps your teenage daughter refuses to attend her grand-parents' fiftieth anniversary party. "I'm not sitting around all night with a bunch of old people!" She's decided to be as sullen and unpleasant as possible. Time to do battle? Nope. Let it go. Leave her home. She's the one losing out. Why drag her against her will and ruin everybody's evening? The grandparents (who are also parents, remember) will understand and likely laugh about it. Go without her, have fun, laugh at her behind her back, and realize that this behavior is definitely a rude, selfish, and stupid teenage strike for independence, but, again, not exactly life-threatening.

Feel free to comment to your teens about your feeling on such behaviors if you must, but in most cases detached bemusement is a better choice. When teens feel confident that they are pissing you off, it only makes it all the more fun and more likely to continue. We know teens love their big drama, but big drama requires two sides in a disagreement, and frankly, if you won't fight back, after awhile they simply lose interest. In fact, after thinking it over on their own, they may even go wash their hair or actually call and apologize to their grandparents.

Picking Your Battles #2: When to Go to War

In the olden days, when your children were, well, children, their lives were an open book. Well sometime between then and now, that book snapped shut, didn't it? Probably right in your face. No matter how open and wonderful you might believe your relationship with your teen to be, all teenagers have secret lives to some extent. Generally speaking, this is best for both teens and parents. They don't want you to know everything and you know what? You don't really want to know everything, either. You may think you do, but you really don't.

However.

You're their parent. Whether they want you to pull rank on them is another story. Ultimately, it's tough luck for them.

Health and Safety

Health and safety come first. When this is an issue, you not only have the "right" to go there, you have the "responsibility."

When you come across a situation which requires waging war, try to remember that our teenagers are still growing in mind and body. They simply do not have the wisdom or life experience to understand the long-term ramifications of idiotic behavior. And keep in mind that although teenage idiotic behavior is a daily event; war doesn't have to be.

Some non-negotiables between you and your teen might include:

1. Drinking and drug use
2. Sexual activity
3. Violence
4. School issues

Fourteen-year-old Macy has party plans this evening. Her parents have asked all the important questions: who will be there, where is it, will there be alcohol/drugs used? The answer Macy, and every other teen, has given is, "No, Mom" with a big sigh of disgust. (You can be certain there will be drugs/alcohol at *every* teen party unless you live in Utah.) Macy is either lying or ignorant. But that's not the issue here. The issue is Macy's safety. Therefore, this situation has the potential to be a legitimate battle worth fighting.

"We tried to be the cool parents, the ones who allowed their daughter

to go to a party even though we suspected there would be drinking.

That is until she got into a drunk-driving accident with two other kids

in the car. We're not the cool parents anymore."

—Jackie

Macy's parents have a plan of their own. They have a no drugs/alcohol policy, and while dropping Macy off her father reminds her that he will be checking in with Macy via cell. If she does not answer, her father will be there within minutes to pick her up and make an embarrassing scene in front of her very cool friends, who would then quickly become her very cool ex-friends. Macy has never failed to answer her phone . . . and odds are she never will.

When you choose to go to battle with your teenager over any issue, you must be very clear with yourself and with them about the following:

- What is the specific issue?
- Why am I concerned enough to go to battle?
- What will be the consequences of the teen's choices/ behavior?

Finally, err on the side of safety. If you have a bad feeling about a situation, shut it down. This is where the phrase "Better safe than sorry" comes into play. Kids won't die if they hear the word "No" once in awhile. But sadly, they may die if they don't. In the end, you always reserve the right to say, "Sorry, kid, not gonna happen."

Phrases Your Parents Used on You That No Longer
Work, Not Even a Little Bit, On Today's Teens:

- "Because I said so."
- "As long as you live under my roof, you'll follow my rules."
- "When I was your age, I . . ."
- "This will hurt me more than it hurts you."
- "Just wait till your father gets home!"
- "That's it! You're going to bed without supper!"
- "Don't waste that food! There are starving people in China!"
- "I used to have to walk to school in a blinding snow-storm! Uphill both ways!"
- "You need how much? I used to be able to get a full meal, plus dessert, tax, and tip, for five dollars!"
- "Someday you'll have kids! Then you'll see!"

Understanding (and Surviving) Peer Pressure

Peer pressure. We know what it means—that your teen's bad-seed friends want your precious little angel to go over to the dark side, tempting her like the snake with the apple in the Garden of Eden. And the parental refrain is well known: if your friends all jumped off a bridge, would you do it? It's all so simple. Or is it?

Actually, peer pressure isn't reserved for teenagers. Maybe you can relate. Francine, a mother of three teens, was recently in the supermarket when she bumped into a parent she knew from school. This mother examined Francine's cart and was stunned to see that Francine was not buying organic milk.

Through her tight, disapproving smile, she told Francine about all the hormones in nonorganic foods and suggested that Francine "Google it" and do some research on what she was feeding her family. Francine was plagued with self-doubt. Was she a bad mother? Was she making poor choices? Was this woman going to tell all the other mothers about Francine's lack of commitment to organic foods? Feeling the heat, Francine quickly jumped off the organic milk bridge.

For teenagers, their peers are everything and the pressure to fit in can be overwhelming. As a rule, teenagers are pack animals. They want what everyone else has, they want to fit in, look the same, feel the same, all in the name of being safe, accepted, and valued. Later, becoming an individual at all costs will become their priority. But not yet.

In order to have some understanding about what your teens are up against in the eyes of their peers, ask questions. These can cover a variety of teenage peer pressure pulse points including sex, drugs, relationships, media, trends, style, school rules, social events, and cliques. Find out what their friends think, say, and do. This is an effective method of gathering information because teens are quite happy to gossip about what "other people" are doing as long as the spotlight isn't shining on them.

"I told my parents I wanted a BlackBerry because all my friends had BlackBerries. They said 'Oh, right, keeping up with the Joneses.' I don't even know anybody named Joneses."

—Maddie, 17

Pop Quiz!

Every single night fourteen-year-old Jenna is contacted constantly on a variety of communication devices: e-mail, texting, cell phone, Facebook. She has endless consultations back and forth with an entire group of girls about:

1. World peace?
2. Curing cancer?
3. Global warming?
4. What to wear tomorrow?

Answer: Well, duh.

To adults this may seem like a ridiculous waste of time, but at fourteen Jenna's entire world is impacted by these consults. You could buy her the outfit shown on the cover of *Seventeen* magazine and she would tell you that it's totally wrong and ugly and geeky and "No one at my school would wear that!" Take a deep breath, because your teenager is telling you, "You are old. You are unfashionable. You know nothing. Please leave my room!" Take the hint. Swallow your pride, and get the hell out of her room. The bottom line is, it doesn't matter what *you* think. It matters what *she* thinks. And she'll know what she thinks just as soon as her friends tell her.

Next stop: Seventeen-year-old Michael is making arrangements for senior prom. He is taking his girlfriend of about a year and he plans to spend the night with a bunch of other teens in a hotel room post-prom. Michael's father thinks this is inappropriate and says no. Michael is furious, and launches into the full teenage litany, "You're treating me like a kid! You can't control me!" Blah, blah, blah, and then Michael utters the magic teenage words, "Everybody else's parents said yes!"

As parents, we know this isn't the point. But in Teen-Town, being an outcast is the very bottom of the food chain. When Michael's father realizes that Michael is dealing with peer pressure, he takes a breath and reacts a bit differently. He asks Michael questions about the details of this hotel plan and after some further discussion, the two of them come to an agreement that allows Michael to save face with his friends, paint his father as "the bad guy," and still maintain a degree of appropriateness suitable to his family's rules. Prepare yourself to be the "bad guy" in all sorts of peer pressure situations. It's a lifesaver in protecting your teen's image with their peers while still holding your teenager to the family values you believe in.

Peer pressure is a lifelong situation, but for teens it can become self-defining and destroying. Keep in mind that at this age everything is "so intense." (It's not, of course, but it feels that way.) Being, or at least feeling, judged is never fun, at any age, and without the maturity and life experience that comes with adulthood your teen will become easily overwhelmed. But stick with them, explain why you're doing what you're doing, and hopefully when your teen is an adult maybe they'll have the confidence to stand up to the organic bully in the supermarket.

CHAPTER 3

you're not leaving the house looking like that!

Although doctors tell us the human skull fully hardens at eighteen months, sometimes even by eighteen years it seems like these kids are still soft in the head. Some of the things teenagers think are okay are just so not. At times, their choices will be baffling, at other times they will be disappointing, but most times they will be just plain old scary. And they make us wonder who in our own gene pool was so deficient to have passed that one down.

Because they're still young, they don't have control over much yet. But, if they do have control over anything, it's themselves. And that starts with how they look. From head (hair color, length, style, to gel or not to gel, that is the question) to toe (boots vs. UGGs vs. flats, learning to walk in heels, and of course only the *right* sneakers will do) and everyplace in between, teens have more decisions to make than the sense to make them.

That's where you come in! (If you dare.) Yes, you're here to help! Just remember, no good deed goes unpunished!

The Teen Wardrobe/Disrobe

In "the olden days" (which according to fourteen-year-old Melanie means anything further back than 2000), teens were embarrassed just to have parents, much less be seen with them in public. But nowadays the parents are the ones who are embarrassed to be seen in public with their teens. This, of course, is because of the way they dress. Once upon a time, college students actually got out of their pajamas to go to class, baseball caps were worn facing forward, and underwear was actually worn underneath clothing. Imagine that. Those nutty olden days!

Exhibit A: Melanie, 14
Good morning Melanie! She is dressed for school today, wearing a red "Playboy Bunny" tank top, a pink bra with straps carefully arranged for maximum viewing, skinny jeans so tight she's guaranteed to get a yeast infection, huge furry UGG boots, and when she bends over to pick up her backpack her thong underwear shows nicely.

Exhibit B: Donald, 16
Hello Son! Donald is dressed for school today in black jeans so big and baggy that his entire carpool could share one pair. He is wearing a belt, but it's wrapped around his groin, instead of his waist, so his bright blue boxers are on clear display. His sneakers sport a bloody red skull and crossbones design.

"My friends and I all wear the same hair and clothes and makeup so we'll be different from anybody else, except for each other."

—Alana, 15

Don't these fashion choices make school uniforms look positively spiffy by comparison? Parents look at their teenagers and wonder: are these clothes? Is this fashion? Is it appropriate? Forget "Can my kid get into trouble for wearing that?" Now it's "Can I get into trouble for allowing my kid to wear that? Are they going to take my kids away? And if so, would I mind?" A generation ago, Melanie would have been labeled a slut and Donald may very well have been considered homeless. But as embarrassing as these choices may be, the sad truth is that once Melanie arrives at school she is going to look exactly like 90 percent of her friends and Donald's pants may actually seem a size too small among his peers as he shuffles to his locker.

You and your teenager are never going to agree on what's stylish and what's fashionable. You are old and they are young; they know everything and you know nothing; they have hair and you don't, and so on. They will insult your wardrobe and let you know your taste in clothes, frankly, sucks. But, to be fair (if only for a moment), remember that style is all relative to the times. To prove this point, look at your very own ninth-grade yearbook picture, and what do you see? Hello, legwarmers! Are you wearing red corduroy culottes, or enormous shoulder pads? Or perhaps purple painter's pants or too tight leggings with brightly colored socks? Are you dressed like Madonna in the '80s, Alex P. Keaton, or Vanilla Ice? Okay then, so before you rip into your teen's poor style choices, think back to all the arguments with your own parents when you were a teenager. Remember that satin roller skating jacket you had to have in the sixth grade but your mother said it was trashy? Well, a dash of humor works better than glaring insults. So when your daughter shows up in a skirt smaller than a washcloth, just tell her that you hope she only paid half-price for that half a skirt. You might get a laugh and she might get the point. But she'll wear it anyway.

Certainly in some fashion selections, you will need to guide your teenager toward acceptable and appropriate, say wearing a jacket when it's twenty-one degrees outside or insisting that their cleavage need not be on display during their Bat Mitzvah. Expect them to protest that they look like a giant grape in their coat and that the Bat Mitzvah dress you like is babyish, but on these occasions feel free to insist. There are occasions in which to be trendy and there are occasions in which to be classy. (Insert lecture on the difference between the two here.) You may recall the uproar a few years back when a group of honor students met the President, and while most of them chose to dress appropriately, many of the girls wore flip-flops. We hope that you will teach your teenager that flip-flops are not appropriate attire for a White House visit, unless you're invited to take a dip in the pool.

Hair Today, Gone Tomorrow (You hope!)

Remember crew-cuts, pompadours, flat-tops, flips, and bobs? Well then your kids are right, you are old! Like everything else, hairstyles change with the generations, and today's teenagers continue to push the envelope as they search for even more variety. Look around the high school courtyard and you'll see neon pink hair, green tipped Mohawks, bleached blonde dreadlocks, and even semibald heads with logos or letters shaved into their scalps. How can you prevent your teenager from becoming one of those kids who decides to abuse their hair in the spirit of fashion or rebellion? Well—you can't.

With any luck their school has a "normal hair" policy that lets you off the hook. Yes of course you can do "the parent thing" and warn, nag, beg, threaten, or bribe. But in the end (split, probably), it's their hair so just take a page out of their playbook and roll your eyes. If your teenager has gone wacky with their hair, they will definitely want to flaunt it in front of you to get a reaction, what with that being the point and all. Don't fall for it. Instead, torture them by giving them a disinterested reaction, "Hmm, did you do something with your hair?"

Some girls dye their shoes to match their prom dress. Kendra, seventeen, decided to take this idea one step further with a haircut for the upcoming prom. She returned home with her head shaved bald and her scalp colored a lovely lavender shade to match her dress. If this happens to you, just smile and get out your videocamera, because with any luck it might win the $10,000 prize on *America's Funniest Home Videos*.

Marco, fourteen, was totally into reggae music and decided to copy the dreadlocks made famous by Bob Marley. However, he took it one step further (don't they always?) and pulled the braids atop his head in a cascading ponytail. Maybe not a big deal on the streets of New York or San Francisco, but in Missoula, Montana, where he lives, he was known as the Boy with the "dreaded locks."

If the disinterested approach doesn't work, here are a few other options to help parents deal:

- *Annoy them:* tell them what they have done is "tame" compared to what you did when you were a teen.
- *Embarrass them:* style your hair to match theirs, no matter how severe.
- *Horrify them:* call whatever they have done "adorable."

In the end, remember that even the most stylish of haircuts is often mocked when it's past its prime. Do you recall the Dorothy Hamill, the Farrah, or the Rachel? How about the enormous afro of the 1970s, the 1980's mullet ("business in the front, party in the back!") or the stringy rattail? All of these spawned major trends, gracing magazine covers and coiffed heads across America. Chances are you might even have been the proud owner of one of these hairstyles yourself. (C'mon, you know you were.)

Some teenagers do wonderful things with their hair, including growing it out and then cutting it to donate it to Locks of Love, a charity that produces wigs. Or perhaps they might shave their heads not in protest, but as an act of support for a friend who lost their hair while battling cancer. Hair options for teens run the gamut from the terrible to the terrific, but regardless of what your teen chooses to do, take a deep breath and remember that hair is a renewable resource and it will either grow back, grow out, or your teen will simply grow up. Plus their birthday is coming up and you've noticed a sale on really big hats . . .

Makeup or War Paint?

Is there really a difference? In many ways, for teenage girls the very choice to wear makeup could be construed as an act of war against good taste. Get ready to see your child's angelic face spackled in blue sparkle eyeshadow and bright pink blush (AKA "The Clown") or painted up with dark black eyeliner and bright red lipstick (AKA "The Bar Fight") because no matter what style your daughter chooses you can expect that your teen or preteen's foray into makeup is going to be an experiment in the hideous. Put on your wrinkle cream, ladies, you've got a whole lot of cringing to do!

Despite a growing trend to sell products to both sexes, most boys have no interest in makeup unless they need to cover a pimple before a big date. If this is the case, offer your concealer and some assistance. If you have a son who is choosing to wear makeup for shock value or other metro-sexual issues, don't immediately freak out (as a parent you automatically reserve the right to freak out later). Find out why your son is interested in wearing makeup. He could just be a major KISS fan.

Even if you escape having to deal with makeup with your son, odds are you won't be so lucky with your daughter. Teen-age girls relish the idea of wearing makeup because it makes them feel more grown up. They also believe, despite what your eyes will tell you, that wearing makeup makes them more attractive and desirable to both sexes. The media presents and advertises to teens that the most beautiful women wear makeup and the most desirable men like it, so in order to compete in the world they must participate. This message starts very early with "pretend" Barbie makeup. And while you can choose to not buy the "pretend" Barbie makeup for your six-year-old, there is no choice with your fourteen-year-old, who can either borrow it from friends, buy it herself, or swipe it from you (or the local drugstore).

"Our eleven-year-old daughter Rae proudly walked in to show
her mom and me that she had put on a face full of makeup.
She looked like The Joker from *Batman*. She was going out to a
party. I blurted out 'Is it a costume party?' Rae started to cry
and neither she nor her mom spoke to me for two days."

—Todd

Be prepared that when you tell your teen that she is more
beautiful without all that black gunk on her eyes, she will
roll those Amy Winehouse eyes in disgust. And if you forbid
her from leaving the house looking like a hooker, she'll just
wash her face, stash the goods in her purse, and put it all
right back on in the school bathroom (she's goooooooood!). So
when faced with this dilemma, what's a parent to do? Teflon-
coat her face so nothing will stick to it? Let's try something
else first and see how that goes.

If your little Tinker Bell wants to look like Tammy Faye,
lay down the law. Designate an age at which she can start
wearing makeup and under what circumstances she'll be
allowed to wear it. For example, you may allow your thirteen-year-old to wear makeup to a dance or party, but not to
school or soccer practice. Also insist upon final approval of
all makeup colors to guarantee a natural look. Then, ask a
friend or well-liked (and uber-patient) relative to give her a
makeup lesson or take her to the beauty counter at a depart-
ment store and let a professional do it. Do yourself a favor
and keep your distance from this learning curve. As your
young teen gets older and enters high school, the natural
look may give way to something totally unnatural with dark

shadows and thick liner. That's when the Teflon idea may come into play.

Teenagers have some crazy ideas about their self-image (go figure) and what makes them look and feel more attractive. Dealing with teens and makeup can be an ugly business and this is one of those times when it's best for parents to step aside, let them play their little reindeer games, and take solace in the fact that "Beauty is in the eye of the beholder." And if they go totally off-track with their makeup, they'll become so unrecognizable that no one will know that they're yours, and you won't have to deal with any embarrassment.

You Pierced *What*?

Body piercing may be something painful, but it's nothing new. In fact, it's as old as man. The oldest mummified man, to be exact. He was named "Otzi the Iceman," making him sound like a character from *The Sopranos*, and was found in a Valentina Trujillon glacier sporting an ear piercing. No word on whether it was in the "right is wrong" or "left is right" ear. Biblical days were no different. In Genesis 24, Abraham has his servant give a nose ring to his daughter-in-law Rebekah. And in Exodus 32, when Aaron makes the golden calf, he makes it out of melted earrings. And since they've been piercing noses in India since the 1500s, they're probably all pierced by now.

In modern times, piercing (places you can see and can't see) was reintroduced by the gay leather subculture in the 1960s, and popularized later as part of the new wave/punk rebellion. Today of course body piercing has become more common, if not outright mainstreamed. Young people in general and teenagers in particular see it (along with its cousins, tattoos and fascinatingly severe hair designs) as a lifestyle choice, a way to express their individuality. And if it happens to royally piss off their parents, well, that's just a bonus.

Piercings are really harmless body ornaments, especially the ones that don't show. Plus, they close up (except for cartilage such as the nose and ear) later. Although nose piercings are the least sanitary and should be avoided if at all possible, in general piercings tend to have minimal infection issues when administered correctly. So you might be better off facilitating this process than trying to shut it down.

Case Study: Daddy X

In order to shed some additional light on to how to handle the piercing predicament, let's turn this section over to a man we will simply call "Daddy X." He's a single father who volunteered to tell his story but did not wish to be identified since his approach to this topic puts him squarely in the minority of parents. Maybe even completely alone. But his philosophy and experience are worth considering, especially given his poignant conclusion. And even if you won't consider it, it's still an interesting read!

My daughter Chloe is a good kid. Back when her eighteenth birthday was approaching I asked her what she wanted. I thought she would say "Justin Timberlake" or "A Porsche" or "Justin Timberlake in a Porsche." What she said instead surprised me: she wanted to get her tongue pierced. I realize most parents would have just ended the conversation then and there and told their teen to get serious. But she was serious.

I suppose I could have played the "You'll do what I say until you're eighteen" card, and she would have respected that. But I knew if I said no without a good reason—and I didn't have one— Chloe was going to get her tongue pierced on her eighteenth birthday. I had this image of her sneaking off late at night into some dirty little piercing parlor inhabited by dirty little piercing people and it just gave me the heebie-jeebies. So I thought about it. And what I thought was, hey it's her tongue. And, unlike tattoos, a tongue piercing is on the inside, where it doesn't show, and it's also not permanent. So, down the road when she grows up and comes to her senses and realizes it's stupid to have a piece of metal in her mouth, she can just pop that sucker out and it'll quickly heal and it's all over. And it's a lot cheaper than a Porsche! So I hatched a plan. I would take Chloe to get her tongue pierced. That way she could do her rebelling thing, and I could be in charge!

We went to a place I found in the yellow pages that sounded safe enough, but when we met the piercer, he was straight out of central casting for Tommy Lee's biopic! Spiked hair, tattoos every- where. Then he pulled out a needle that must have been a foot long. Chloe's eyes got very big, like they did when she was a little girl at the pediatrician's office about to get a shot. Tommy Lee, wear- ing rubber gloves, applied some anesthetic and then used forceps to extend Chloe's tongue, then pushed the gigantic needle through it. I just gasped. It looked like some sort of magic trick, my "little girl" standing there with this needle through her tongue. Ouch, that hurt! Hurt me, that is. Chloe was fine. Then Tommy Lee removed the needle, inserted a stud in the new hole, and screwed in the bottom half. And then it was over. Later Chloe's tongue swelled up big and she couldn't really talk for two days, so the cell phone savings pretty much paid for the piercing.

That was nearly two years ago. Chloe still has the piercing. And although this will sound strange, I'm glad we did it together. It had been a long time since she was little and I took her to the park and to ballet and youth soccer, and I'm glad this was a "we" thing that we still talk (and laugh) about sometimes! And I think it made me realize Chloe is not just a kid and not just a teen. Those things are temporary. She's my daughter, and I'm her father, and I love her whether she has a piece of metal in her tongue or not. Those things are permanent. We are in this life journey together, and I know doing this with her was better for us than saying "No!" would have been.

Tat's Ridiculous: Think Before You Ink

Tattoo Rule #1: If you are dead set against your teens getting tattoos, whatever you do don't tell them. Since many of their activities are designed to separate themselves from you (AKA rebel), the very idea that you don't want them to do this will guarantee that they will. Unfortunately it doesn't work in reverse, so forget the "I forbid you to clean your room!" gambit, although props to you for thinking of it.

Tattoo Rule #2: If you or your spouse has a tattoo, forget Rule #1 since you will be unable to stop your teens from getting one. Or more. That whole "Do as I say, not as I do" lesson went out with the Partridge Family.

Tattoo Rule #3: Okay, there is no Tattoo Rule #3. But if you are open to your teens becoming tattooed, or even if you're not but believe they might do it anyway, there are some precautions you can take.

Whereas piercings are simple (a hole in the ear is a hole in the ear is a hole in the ear), tattoos are far more complicated thanks to all the variables involved. If your older teen starts to make noise about getting a tattoo, it's time to start asking questions. Round up the usual suspects: Who, What, Where, How, and Why. "Who" will be doing the tattooing? "What" will the tattoo be of? "Where" on the body will it be located? "How" big a tattoo are we talking about? And last (but certainly not least) "Why?"

"Who?"

In the United States, there are more tattoo artists than policemen. Okay maybe not, but doesn't it feel that way? It may not always be easy to find a cop when you need one, but on every block there's someone just waiting to give you a tattoo. Maybe the war on crime could be won if we just deputized all the tattoo artists—okay, bad idea. But yes, they ARE artists. They are literally creating art on the skin. And while you may like art in general, do you like *every* artist? Of course not. So remember, just because they may have a license and a needle doesn't necessarily mean they have talent. For this job, they will need all of the above. So, just like any other craftsman, you'd want to see samples of their work first.

"What?"

Most people have contemplated the question "If you got a tattoo, what would it be of?" Expect your male teen to go the "bad-ass" route, either with incendiary words or images like flaming skulls. Female teens will likely care more about something cute, like fairies, butterflies, Asian symbols, and shamrocks. Don't get too worked up over the "What" unless it's something destined to get them hurt like "Kill the Police," "Punch Me Here, I Dare You," or "Biker Gangs Don't Scare Me."

"Where?"

This is an important one. A "Life Sux" tattoo on the butt is bad enough, but if it's on the forehead it could definitely stand in the way of career advancement. However, one modest, strategically placed tattoo on a wrist or ankle isn't exactly cause for an intervention. Other popular locations include the top of the feet, the lower back, and the back of the neck, which is handy-dandy because it can always be covered by hair, if your teen hasn't shaved his/her head.

"How?"

Meaning, how big will this thing be? Which really means, make sure you can hide it.

"Why?"

Finally, the biggie. Odds are the answer to this one will be either "Because they're cool" or "I dunno" or maybe just a grunt. All might be stupid, in that lovably stupid teenage way of theirs, but in a sense all are valid to their way of thinking, or nonthinking as the case may be.

Here's why it makes sense to have this involved conversation about tattooing with your teen. For starters, few things in life are as difficult (or unpleasant) to undo as a tattoo. Putting the toothpaste back into the tube would be a breeze compared to the involved laser removals needed to make it all go away. And even then they don't always work perfectly, which is why many people prefer tattooing over an existing, unwanted tattoo (e.g., "Jason & Jessica 4Ever," when "4Ever" arrived a bit sooner than expected) with a new one.

But the best reason for going down this road is this: in TeenTown, very often thinking about things is the same as actually doing them. Translation: having the idea to get a tattoo, and knowing what it would be of and where it would be located, is actually close enough without getting one. In a sense, they live vicariously through themselves! That's why it's good to do the following:

- Take them to a tattoo parlor. They may love the idea of the tattoo, and maybe even the threat of the tattoo, but no way most of these softies have any interest in the actual pain of a tattoo. So show them the blood as the needle rips into someone's skin and find out the risk of infection. Chat about how there's no going back once you start the tattoo, no matter how excruciatingly painful it may be (even they will agree that a half-finished tattoo is worse than no tattoo at all).

- Take them to a laser removal facility. Talk to people in the waiting room who now realize how stupid it was to get a tattoo, the process they have to undergo to remove it, and how much it costs to have it removed. Then tell your teen there's no way in hell you're paying for it!

- Have them check out a tattoo on an older person. Some tattoos look cool on a teenager, but not so much next to wrinkles and liver spots.

> "I was telling my sister about the tattoo I wanted to get someday, and our dad overheard us and told us about the tattoo HE wanted to get someday. It was the first time I started to suspect that he might be secretly cool."
>
> —Amber, 17

And after all that, if you're still not winning this battle, tell your teen they can have their tattoo—and you'll be there to hold their hand while they get it. Odds are, at this point they will change the subject and want to know what there is to eat. Congrats. Your work here is done.

CHAPTER 4

what we have here is a failure to communicate

Sometimes the only difference between talking to your teen and talking to a wall is that you can understand why the wall doesn't listen because it of course lacks ears. Teens have ears, and while they tend to hear they also tend not to listen, and faster than you can say "You're not going out tonight until that room is clean!" you find yourself in one of a seemingly endless series of battles that include slamming doors, storming out, and the muttering of profanities. And that's just what you're doing!

So given the previously discussed existence of TeenSpeak (the official language of TeenTown), stop for a moment and stare in wide wonder. You used to speak this language (or at least an outdated version of it) yourself when you were a teen. And yet, now that you have teens of your own, it's Greek to you (unless you actually speak Greek, in which case it's Portuguese or Russian or Tagalog or something like that).

Understand, grasping TeenSpeak is not primarily about deciphering and speaking the current, hip (or whatever the hip word is nowadays for "hip") version of words you already know. It's not about understanding what your teen is saying . . . it's about understanding what your teen is *trying* to say. And, conversely, understanding how to make them understand that you in fact understand. Understand? Let's not try to explain it—let's just do it!

The A-to-Zs of How to Talk So Your Teen Will Listen

Always begin sentences with the word "Dude" to get their attention.

Be careful not to say anything important to them while they're eating, since science has proven that their ears and mouths cannot be open at the same time.

Cash talks. And no matter the generation, it knows TeenSpeak. No teen alive will turn down money, even if they have to do you-know-what to get it.

Don't use multisyllabic words. Teens have short attention spans and tend to stop listening after one syllable.

Everyone likes to be complimented. Like chocolate, a compliment releases something good in the brain. So if you want the garage cleaned, try "Hi honey, your skin has really cleared up! Please clean the garage."

Forego subtlety. When you drive past laborers sweating in the summer sun, remind your teens, "That's what happens when you don't stay in school." If you see an old person with a stooped back, tell them, "That's what happens when you don't drink milk." If you come across homeless people, be sure to say, "Be thankful for what you have." These are the things they will remember.

Great minds think alike. Before you correct, connect. If (when) they mess up, say, "I can see why you thought that way," or "I would have thought that too," or "When I was your age I made that same mistake." This way, they get reminded that you're in this family thing together, and you make your point without diminishing them. You don't want to diminish them—you just want to diminish their mind-bogglingly bad choices.

Here's something to try when they have done something bone-headed. Even if they're upset in the moment, you can cut the tension by telling them that next time, before they make a decision they should ask themselves: "What Would Fergie Do?"

If you want to strike them with fear, start a conversation with "We need to talk." If you don't, then don't.

Joke around with them. You are always their parent but you don't always have to be their keeper, their boss, their warden. Keep things light when you can. Try going around using "their language." Instead of "Hi honey," greet them with "What it is, gangsta?"

Know what's hard for them and what's easy for them. That will allow you to know when they need a kick in the butt and when they need a hug.

Let them slide sometimes. Let an obvious offense go unpunished and undiscussed (but do make it clear it did not go unnoticed). This nonverbal communication tells them that ultimately you're in this together, and they will propbaby appreciate it. It may also throw them for a bit of a loop, which is a nice bonus!

Minimize use of your "angry voice." Even dogs know intonation, and the last thing you want is for your teen to get defensive. Okay, the last thing you want is a colonoscopy, but the next-to-last thing you want is for your teen to get defensive.

Never be afraid to apologize. They will see it for what it is, a sign of strength, not weakness. It will mean something because you're the parent—no one can make you do it. Again, you're building a foundation of trust and communication here. The stronger the foundation, the more it can withstand. So if you lose it a little bit, and you will, go back afterwards and say you're sorry. It helps if you mean it, but even if you don't, do it anyway.

Organize your thoughts before a big talk. Otherwise when you get into their room, all you're going to be able to think about are the towels on the floor and last month's meatloaf on a plate peeking out from under the bed and about how you could just put a sign reading "Garbage Museum" on their door and install a turnstile and charge admission. And you'll totally forget what you went in there to talk to them about in the first place.

Prior to reading them the riot act, give them a chance to explain their side of the situation. It's an opportunity for you to realize what they were thinking (or not thinking, as the case may be), and there's a great chance that by hearing their own flimsy rationale and excuses they will be able to realize where they went wrong—and will hopefully go right in the future. A parent can always dream, can't they?

Quit nagging them over every little thing. Did your parents do that to you? Of course, and did you hate it? If you find fault on a regular basis about the little stuff, your teens are less likely to take it to heart when you come to them to talk about the big stuff.

Role-playing is a great way to shake things up from time to time. If you always give the same speech, always under the same circumstances, rest assured they will always tune you out faster than you can turn off that rap crap on their CD players. Next time go in there and role-play. You be the teen and let your teen be you. If you both really get into it, you'll learn to look at life through both sides now. And it should be good for a laugh.

Spend leisure time with them. Join them in front of the TV. Let them control the remote. Ask them questions about what you're watching. Find out their opinions. Get to know them as people. Because that's what they are, or at least will be once you're finished teaching them how. And the better your bond during peacetime, the fewer and farther between the wartimes will be.

Teach them piglatin. Like real Latin, it's a dead language. But unlike real Latin, it's fun. The only other chance they'll get to learn it is if you send them to a swanky expensive private college and they offer it as a course, along with whittling and kite-flying. Hey, teach them now and they'll make Dean's List! Once they have learned, insist on PLO (piglatin only) conversations, particularly in public places.

U should learn to speak the teen's version of Morse Code—the language of Instant and Text Messaging. These include the standard LOL, OMG, and ASAP, as well as the less common (but more important) POS (Parent Over Shoulder). With a complete list and a little practice, you'll be able to say NW (No Way), YGTBKM (You've Got To Be Kidding Me), and SMHID (Scratching My Head In Disbelief) without wasting time on actual words, which you can save for other adults.

Very often you might look at your seventeen-year-old and still see a seven-year-old with car keys and an expensive sushi addiction. Try to treat your teens like semi-adults by including them in some semi-adult conversations—nothing too heavy but topics you might not have shared with them before. These might include issues you are having with work, or an aging parent, or sharing some insights you have obtained during your own life's journey. That fundamental shift can be invaluable to you both as your relationship starts to transition.

Whispering speaks louder than yelling. Sure, that lacks logic. But in a world where Paris Hilton is an international superstar for no good reason (no good reason), anything is possible if not downright likely. Yelling backs people away. Whispering makes them come closer. Less volume, more communication.

Xylophone. No, this is not a pathetic attempt at finding something that begins with the letter X. Well maybe it is, so what? The other twenty-five letters aren't enough? Maybe your teens are right about you, you are harsh!

Yank a board game out of the closet out of the blue, dust it off, and challenge your teen. Checkers, chess, Parcheesi, anything that doesn't run on batteries and has no video. Odds are they'll try to plug it in, but before you're finished there's a good chance your other kids will fight to get in on the action before it's over. Tell them long stories about how you used to play with your parents and/or siblings when you were a kid. And while they're busy yawning, you can cheat.

Zen is perhaps the best philosophy in terms of communicating with teenagers. You can read a book about it if you like, but it's probably easier and faster to simply buy a box of fortune cookies and share them every night after dinner. Make yours sound like the solution to all the mysteries of the universe. Your teens will do it too. Compliment their reading, and then tell them to clear the table. If you're truly Zen, even if they refuse, it won't bother you. Sort of a like a philosophical Prozac.

"It goes both ways." Coincidentally, so does this. Time to turn this thing around. Your teen wants to talk. Just not to you. So let's reverse this alphabetical thing with 26 ways to help that. (Assuming you want it helped. If you believe that teens should be endured and not heard, skip to the next section. Hey, it's a choice.)

Talking is an action that appears active. Listening, on the other hand, is an action that appears passive. So in this case "how to listen" means creating an atmosphere between you and your teen that will encourage communication, hopefully beyond the usual grunts and one-word answers.

The A-to-Zs of How to Listen So Your Teen Will Talk

Zoom in on your teen's fears/insecurities behind their ridiculous requests. When they ask to throw a party for 200 at your house ("We'll just be in the yard, nothing will get broken") recognize they're not hopelessly insane, they just want to be popular with their peers and this is sadly the best idea they could come up with. Maybe you could come up with a better idea (since you couldn't do any worse!) that still gives them what they want without giving you the opportunity to find out if you really have enough homeowner's insurance.

Yelling is the worst way to get your point across, and it's never too soon to teach your teen the same thing. If they yell at you, whatever you do don't yell back. Instead be the grownup and simply tell them you can either have a yelling contest (which is about volume) or a conversation (which is about content). You'll be right, they'll recognize that, and in typical teen fashion they'll hate you for it. But it'll pass.

Xylophone. Okay, yes, this is a pathetic attempt at finding something that begins with the letter X. Deal with it.

When your teen has a problem (which will be roughly 100 percent of the time) and they ask your advice about it (which will be roughly 1 percent of the time), never actually offer advice. Sit down with them—literally—and listen, then use your experience to offer up what you see as their options. Let them pick their own poison. And if they pick the wrong one, ask them why until they realize they picked the wrong one. It's the difference between handing them a fish and teaching them to fish. And a lot less slimy.

Vindicate your teen whenever possible. Praise them to others when they're around to hear it. "Guess who got a great report card?" "Guess who cleaned the whole garage without complaining?" These events are more unusual than Halley's Comet, so you might as well get the most out of them. (Make sure not to include the crack about Halley's Comet, though, as it tends to defeat the purpose.)

Utter compliments when they tell you things. "That's a good idea." "That's funny." "I'll try that, thanks." It keeps the lines of communication open. And for you, good karma. (It's okay for you to get something out of this too.)

Teens are often told to do things and asked to do things (and then told to do things again since they never do things when asked) but are rarely asked their opinions. Try it. "Which of these do you like better?" Or "Which of these would you like for dinner?" It will make them feel valued at your level. Then do it their way (so make sure either choice is okay with you before you ask!).

Show interest in their lives. If you heard about a situation with one of their friends, follow up on it later and ask "Whatever happened with . . . ?" It will remind them that you're a good listener and that you care about what they do beyond getting a haircut and calling Grandma once in awhile.

Remember the power of nonverbal communication. Smile at your teen, nod when they talk, pat them on the shoulder as you walk past. Bond-builders all, and they don't cost nothin'.

Quirks. We all have them. Some people have lucky coins they carry, some people don't like their food to touch the other food on the plate, and some people insist on starting each day on the same foot every day. Share your quirks with your teen. They'll make you more approachable. (But save the really really weird ones, they don't need to think you're some kind of freak. Even if you are. Especially if you are.)

Problem solving is a good skill for adults, but it doesn't translate directly to teens very well. When they complain about everyday teen-type issues, don't be in a hurry to try and make everything okay for them. Advice is great, but sometimes just being there and listening are better.

Once your teen does open up for a chat, you will find that sometimes their stories wander more aimlessly than Johnny Appleseed criss-crossing the country planting trees. Don't interrupt, don't try to get your teen focused, don't "cut to the chase." Sometimes what happens before the chase is more important than the chase itself.

Nails, hammer, paint. Build something with your teen. Put on some music. Alternate between theirs and yours. Explain to them how yours is better. Listen to them tell you that you're wrong. Talk more, listen more, repeat. Then take what you made and sell it on eBay. Or stick it on a shelf in your garage.

Make up a "Parent Quiz." Teens hate homework, but this quiz will be different. Maybe twenty-five questions, make them multiple choice. "I was born in which state?" "What was my childhood nickname?" "I played which sports in high school?" "My first kiss was with someone named _____?" First off, don't be shocked how little your kids know you! But then maybe realize they don't know what you don't tell them. Then when they're finished, go over the answers together. They'll have questions!

Let your teen see you fail. Parents often believe they need to be all-knowing pillars of, well, pillariness. And just because you're not supposed to be their "friend" doesn't mean you can't appear human. Do something with them you suck at . . . ice skating, tennis, gardening. If they see you struggle a bit, it will give them permission to struggle a bit too. Which they are going to do anyway. Help them out. Fall on your butt once in awhile.

Knock on their door sometimes for no reason and (after being granted entrance) ask "What are you doing?" Make yourself at home. It IS your home.

Jump in. When they're doing a chore like garage cleanup or car wash, join them and help out. They'll like that, and then at the end try to get them to pay you for a change.

Invite them into the kitchen and then inform them they're cooking dinner. You will be their "sous chef." Start with something simple and if possible "teen-proof." Show them what to do but let them do it. Make sure you have frozen dinners available as a back-up plan if all hell breaks loose.

Hearing happens with the ears. Listening happens with the heart. Sure it sounds like something you would pull out of a fortune cookie. Does that make it wrong?

Get an iPod and use it a lot, especially when your teen wants to ask you for things.

Food is to teens what flowers are to bees. If you're tired of chasing down your "busy" teen to talk to them, go to the kitchen and fry something (anything, as long as it's fried) and they'll come to you faster than you can say "BLT." Which is pretty fast, really.

Encourage some "family time." Teens are hermits waiting to happen and if left to their own devices would brick themselves into their rooms as long as you would promise to slide meals and an occasional DVD under their door. Bring them literally out into family. (You may need to bake cookies or rent a good movie to get this to happen.) Remember that it's important for your teen to talk in general, to others as well as you. Otherwise they live much of their lives up in their heads, and it's pretty scary in there.

Dads should take their sons to lunch at Hooters. Moms should take their daughters. Controversial approach? Maybe. Don't do a preamble, don't explain the lessons you're in the process of teaching. Don't even think about what you want them to learn there. Just do it. By exposing (for lack of a better word) your teens to the real world (albeit in a tame form) you will definitely get them thinking—and talking.

Common ground is a great place to stand together. If you can find some. Odds are you can if you try. Clearly you and your teen have more differences than similarities. But only the specifics have changed. You were a teen once! And odds are you wouldn't go back there again with a time machine on a bet! (Unless it was maybe to save money to eventually buy Google stock.) Tell your teen what your parents were like when you were a teen. They'll dig it.

Back to the Future. Remember when they were smaller and you two had a "thing" you did together on a regular basis? Maybe it was youth soccer, or trips to ballet classes or judo? Maybe your teen has outgrown those things, but that's no reason why you can't discover new things. Find some common ground, whether it be as simple as a TV show you watch together every week, or a Saturday lunch spot. You'd be surprised at how much teens will talk when it doesn't look like you have set things up for a talk!

Ask your teen "How's your life?" Then hang there and let them tell you.

And Now, a Message from Our Sponsors

Even if you get down the ABCs of communicating with your teen, that's only half the battle, because the media speaks to them as well. And often times, you're not happy with what they have to say. What's the latest with celebrity hookups, breakups, and who's in rehab? Which video gets the most hits on YouTube? What's the number one download on i-Tunes? Who is on the cover of this month's *Seventeen* magazine? Do you know? Do you care?

Teenagers know and teenagers care. Teenagers are the ultimate consumers of mass media. The majority of mass media is simply a junk food buffet and most teenagers have an all-you-can-eat attitude. Will your teenager become a serial killer after listening to heavy metal music? Will your daughter demand gastric bypass surgery or develop an eating disorder after viewing image after image of unrealistic female bodies? Not likely, but not a day will go by when your teen is not using some form of media to inform their daily lives, fuel their fantasies, and evaluate their sense of self.

Advertising is of course, and always has been, the biggest culprit in the media empire. Preying on teenager's fears and insecurities, advertisers directly sell to teens with disposable income, telling them to buy this, eat that, own these—and if you do, you will be happier, you will be better looking, and you will get the guy/girl. This is a problem disguised as a solution. Most teenagers are clued into the sales pitch and while they may enjoy the images of barely-there bikinis partying on a beach, they are not quickly sold on the idea that a diet soda will change their lives into one big beach party. Although they might be willing to give it a shot.

The other forms of media are more insidious, because it is literally everywhere your teen looks (which of course is the idea) and whether they believe the hype or not, teens are constantly registering the misleading messages they see, hear, and read. For teenagers, the media can be as big or even a bigger influence on their attitudes and behavior than parents or friends. Virtually nothing the media sells or glamorizes would be a choice you'd make in your home and yet every day your teenager is exposed to wasted celebrities acting like idiots on TMZ, local newscasts filled with crime scenes and scary statistics, sexist and violent music videos on MTV, and real-life fraternity hazing or Girls Gone Wild clips on YouTube. Song lyrics filled with hate speech and foul language, murder and mayhem-laden video games and half-naked women. Your teenager is watching talk shows featuring pedophiles, underage and undereducated mothers, drug overdoses, and eating disorders. Your daughter is reading magazines full of suggestions for better sex lives and gazing at endless photos of surgically altered and airbrushed models. Your son is reading advertisements for drugs to create a bigger and better penis or zoning out while watching college strippers on YouTube. The media is happy to offer teenagers, who are certainly a less than discerning (to put it mildly) audience, their skewed version of reality and teenagers everywhere spend most of their nonschool waking hours consuming it in one form or another.

So What to Do?
You wouldn't allow your teenager to eat at Burger King every day, so why allow them to endlessly devour media messages that can be equally as hazardous to their health and well-being?

Good question. Glad you asked.

Unless you reside in an igloo, and frankly with Wi-Fi, even a community of igloos isn't immune, parents simply cannot prevent or protect their teenagers from the media influence. What parents can do is educate themselves about what's being marketed to our teenagers and discuss with their teens the accuracy and entertainment value of the media. The best you can do is to teach your teenager to view the media's message with a discerning eye. Make them realize the media is trying to use them. Because of course it is.

Now, amongst the junk there is actual art, creativity, and talent to be discovered and appreciated and your teenagers will gravitate toward those things too. Most teens will find significance and deep personal meaning in a particular song, TV show, or movie. They may relate to or idolize a musician, actor, or sports star and you may never have a clue as to why. It doesn't matter. Teenagers are simply looking to connect with the greater world and find understanding and meaning in their young lives. Just like you did back when you didn't know any better.

Pop Quiz!
Are These Actual Mainstream Media Headlines?

Answer yes or no:
1. Reality star fired for cellulite.
2. Kids set homeless man on fire, put video on YouTube.
3. Doomsday cult members emerge after years underground.
4. Octopuses flirt, hold hands.
5. Bush puppet killed on TV show.
6. Transgender man gives birth.

7. Diet Coke causes tumors in rats.
8. Skinny star insists she eats.
9. Third graders plot to kill teacher.
10. Senator facing sex tape scandal.
11. Football star arrested for urinating on dance floor.
12. Woman stuck to toilet seat for two years.
13. Young cancer patient's marijuana stolen.
14. Fans give blood to save vampire show.
15. Teenager receives text message from dead girlfriend.

For the answers, ask your teen!

No Laughing Matter—Serious Teen Issues

Try as hard as you might, there are times when parent/teen talk just doesn't cut it because the issue cuts much too deep. It would be irresponsible to write a book about teenagers without including these serious topics. It would be downright disrespectful to poke fun or be snarky about them. Teens sometimes find themselves dealing with difficult family and self-esteem issues. And while parents hope to shield their adolescents from pain, unfortunately life happens and regardless of good intentions, teenagers can find themselves confronted with adult concerns, such as:

- Death
- Divorce
- Moving
- Stepfamilies
- Parental alcohol or drug abuse
- Family violence

- Physical abuse
- Sexual abuse

Understanding and managing these sorts of life-altering events can impact teenagers with a powerful force. Instances ranging from divorcing parents or an attempted date rape can easily be triggers for teenagers who may find themselves unable to communicate their concerns with family or friends. They are left feeling overwhelmed, anxious, and unable to cope. When teens have trouble coping, they can begin acting out in alarming and disturbing ways. Girls tend to turn their sadness, anger, and frustration inward onto themselves, while boys tend to lash out at the world around them.

Cutting

It is frightening to realize that your child is purposefully doing physical harm to themselves. Cutting is one way teenagers—primarily teenage girls—act out their emotional pain. These girls will attempt to relieve the stress and sadness they feel inside by cutting themselves repeatedly and intentionally with razor blades or scissors or burning themselves with cigarettes, lighters, and matches. Self-mutilation is done in secrecy and the outside scars are almost always on arms or other body parts that can be easily hidden and covered with clothing. If you suspect your teen is participating in cutting, ask to see for yourself and then seek professional help.

Eating Disorders

Teenage girls are also much more likely than boys to develop an eating disorder, such as anorexia or bulimia. Girls who suffer from these types of disorders are looking for something they can control in what may feel to be some sort of out-of-control environment. Girls can become fanatical with their weight and their diet, often talking of nothing else. Some obvious signs of an eating disorder may include extreme starvation and obsessive behaviors around food and exercise. Other symptoms may not be as obvious, but may take shape in the form of strange but ritualistic eating habits, frequent bathroom trips at mealtimes (vomiting) and the abuse of laxatives, and/or binge eating.

One of the many things girls will often say during or after treatment for cutting or eating disorders is that when they are abusing their bodies, the physical damage helps them mask or avoid the pain they are feeling on the inside. If you should see odd wounds or strange eating habits developing, know that these injuries to your teenager's physical body are symptoms of much deeper suffering and your child needs your help.

Depression and Mental Illness

Both teenage boys and girls can find themselves struggling with depression and mental illness. Mental illness can be as simple as an ADHD diagnosis or mild anxiety or as complex as severe bipolar mood shifts or schizophrenia. Left untreated, depression and mental health issues can ultimately be life-threatening. If mental illness has been a problem in your family's history, you may be able to recognize some familiar symptoms and seek early intervention. All parents need to be aware and be willing to acknowledge a sudden or severe change in your teenager's behavior, demeanor, and their normal teenage eating, sleeping, and social habits. If your teenager seems unable to shake off "the black mood," there is something going on beyond a bad day or just feeling bummed out. Teenagers struggling with depression or other forms of mental illness will often attempt to self-medicate using drugs and alcohol. These teens are not "partying," but are withdrawing from a world that is causing them pain.

While teenage girls usually focus their acting-out upon themselves, teenage boys are more likely to confuse their feelings of sadness and pain with anger and hostility and to become verbally or physically abusive toward others to relieve their own stress. Emotionally troubled teenage boys are likely to participate in illegal activities, join gangs of other disenfranchised boys, and be arrested for petty crimes like vandalism and stealing. Do not make the mistake of assuming that "boys will be boys" when you see your son struggling to control his behavior or lashing out in unacceptable ways.

As a parent, if you find yourself struggling to deal with a teenager in distress, there is assistance out there. Do not blame yourself. Do not blame your teenager. Intervene as quickly as possible. Reach out for support. Go to your computer and use a search engine to find online support groups and resources and referrals for professional help right in your hometown. One quick phone call to your child's school, pediatrician, or a local mental health hotline is also a good first step.

CHAPTER 5

papa's got a brand new bag . . . of house rules

Remember those times your teens did everything they were supposed to, when they were supposed to, without being told they were supposed to? Of course you don't, because that never happened. Take the words "How many times do I have to tell you . . . ?" directly out of your vocabulary. They are an auditory illusion. You will swear you can hear yourself saying them, yet they will never be heard. So box them up like third-grade art projects and store them for safekeeping. You won't be needing them again for awhile. The sad fact is that laying down the law is yet another Parental Bottomless Pit. During the teenage years you'll be doing it more often than paying the pizza man.

This doesn't mean you should abandon rules. In fact, this is when you need rules more than ever. Just don't expect them to be followed, and when they are followed be prepared for them to be accompanied by one of your teen's BFFs: the argument, the scowl, or the ever-present eye-roll. So why set rules that won't be followed? Simple. You may think the rules you set down in your household are for your teens, but really they are for your benefit. Rules give parents the illusion of structure, of empowerment, of control during these uncontrollable years. This is denial in its most healthy and beneficial form. Go for it.

Remember how you survived your own adolescence? It was by having your head so far up your own butt that you barely realized there were other people living on the planet at the time. It was all about you. And now you have come full circle. Your teenager's adolescence is, from their perspective, all about them. You will survive it by making it, whenever possible, all about you. You can do this. Time to channel your inner teen. You can do this! Practice by rolling your eyes. **You can do this!**

Chores & Responsibilities

At first blush, it looks like a match made in heaven: you want your teen to do things, and your teen wants to do things. Perfect! But upon closer inspection you'll realize it's actually a match made in a much hotter, pitchfork-infested place. You want your teen to keep their room clean, dump the trash, walk the dog, clear the table, and rake the leaves. Your teen wants to chill, go out, chill, sleep in, and chill. At this point there may be only one thing you can agree upon: someone is making someone else's life a living hell here.

You're thinking, if they just did what they were supposed to, you would leave them alone. They're thinking, if you would just forget about that "do what they're supposed to" stuff and skip straight to the leaving them alone part, that'd work. (By the way, this may be the only time you may hear them using the word "work" in a sentence.)

Parents make excuses all the time for why their teen-agers don't help out: "Susie's major responsibility is her schoolwork," or "oh well, of course I have to remind her, but she does feed the dog." Study after study, statistic after statistic tells us that children and teenagers who partici-pate in family chores and undertake family or community responsibilities are ultimately happier with themselves and their families, have better family values, higher self-esteem, and grow up to become more productive members of soci-ety. If parents make excuses and allow their teenagers to sit back and do nothing but put their hand out every day for a twenty, they'll certainly be happy to go along. But what are they learning about how to live in the world? How to be a lazy, ungrateful sloth? Well, maybe that's a little strong, but you get the idea. So, do your teen a favor and teach—okay, force—them to pitch in and get to work. Fire the gardener, let the dog crap pile up on the lawn, leave the dishes in the sink, close the Daddy ATM, cancel the nanny and the house-keeper—and put your teen to work. Without pay!

Now that we agree your kid should do chores, how do you get them to do them?

Webster's Dictionary offers not only two definitions of the word "chore" but also an insight into the different mind-sets of teens and their parents. Most parents would define "chore" as "a routine job." But ask most teens, and they'll opt for the alternate (glass half-empty) definition: "a diffi-cult or disagreeable task." Just keep in mind that to teens, "work" is a four-letter word . . . and not one of their favorite four-letter words, either. There is no "I" in "work." Or in "chore" for that matter. That is at the heart of teens' problem with chores: they do not directly profit by doing them. Yes, you can always say "You live here too, you can contribute."

And of course you'd be right, but they're not listening. Your best bet is to divide things thusly:

1. Teens must offset their own mess;
2. Regular chores (unpaid);
3. Special jobs over-and-above (paid or otherwise rewarded).

Offsetting Their Own Mess

This is a pretty simple concept. (And one that so perfectly illustrates the phrase "Easier said than done.") For starters, it means containing themselves within their own room. The reality is that your teen's room will only rarely be clean. However, you should insist (nag, nag, repeat) that things like leftover food and overflowing wastebaskets (or whatever else particularly annoys you/offends other members of the house who happen to have noses) be taken care of. Their rooms may be messes, but you are the parent and you have the right to insist that it is not *dirty*.

But better to have their room a mess than your whole house. So this means they are not allowed to leave their clothes, books, backpacks, sports equipment, or any other possessions anyplace but in their rooms (or neatly in an agreed-upon organized common area). If this is an issue in your house, you will be shocked how much better everything will look once they get with the program.

"If my room is messy, why can't my parents just shut the door? Isn't that why rooms have doors?"

—Skye, 16

Second, you'll want them to concentrate on consistently eliminating any evidence of their existence in the common areas of your home. In their favorite room, the kitchen, this means cleaning up their own messes, putting food away, and actually (they can do it!) getting dirty dishes inside the dishwasher and not simply into The Magic Sink (so named because teens believe that anything that finds its way inside magically cleans itself and puts itself away). And finally, there's laundry. If they're older teens, they're old enough to do their own. But make sure to give them a tutorial on the whites vs. colors/hot water vs. cold water vs. dry-clean-only things, otherwise you will be doling out money to replace their ruined wardrobes.

The bad news is that to be fair, you have to do your part here. The good news is, in this case your part is actually to do nothing. Meaning, you have to stop cleaning up after them for a bit until they can get it together. If you continue to clean up after them, and simply tell them to do it the next time, guess what? "Next time" never actually arrives. No one is suggesting you just let them leave their stuff everywhere. But instead of just doing it because "it's easier to just do it myself," call them on it. As in "Are we having a yard sale? Because I saw some sports equipment lying on the front lawn." Or "There are clothes in the TV room—are we starting a Goodwill pile?" Cue the eye-roll. But at least they will carry the offending items into their room, which is where you want them. And if they don't put it away, it actually will be time for a garage sale and to donate their former possessions to Goodwill.

Unpaid Chores
Regular unpaid chores are a good way to remind teens that they are part of something bigger than themselves, in this case the family unit. Keep them simple and few; you don't want to

overload them with selflessness or anything. But also don't be surprised when they don't even handle the little you have given them. Don't make it a fight, but don't let them off the hook either. They may think of it as "nagging" but to you it's just "reminding." Depending upon how many chores and children you are juggling here, you may want to post a written list so they won't be able to use the "No, I don't do that today" excuse, or claim that chore is their little sister's because "we traded." Unpaid chores are never transferable. You are the only one who has the power to reassign chores. That's important unless you want your youngest child doing all your teenager's work for them. Which you don't.

Special Jobs

These beyond-the-call-of-duty jobs should be paid for and doled out as a reward for offsetting their own mess and handling their regular chores. Eventually this may even happen without being asked, but don't hold your breath on that one unless you can hold your breath a very, very, very long time. These jobs might include things you are going to pay someone for anyway (such as having your car washed, snow shoveled, gutters cleaned, and so on). Just make sure your teen knows that if you are going to hire them instead, you are going to hold them to a professional standard. This is a win-win as it'll get the work done, it'll put some money in their pocket, and they will learn a good lesson in a day's pay for a day's work. Technically, that makes it a win-win-win.

Monitoring the Monitor, Part 1: Computers

Can you imagine Ray Bradbury on Facebook? Conceive of George Orwell spending his free time chatting on the *LOST*

fans websites? Or Aldous Huxley surfing porn? Talk about
A Brave New World! The point being, not even the greatest
science fiction writers of the twentieth century could have
predicted what has become the wildest science fiction experiment of all time, the Internet.

Kids as young as six years old are "Googling" for information. Rosie, age seven, heard her teenage sister use the
word "lesbian" and decided to "Google" it. Well, after finding the text hard to understand, she clicked on "images" and
she sure got an eyeful, as well as the "You're not old enough
yet" dismissal from mom.

For today's teenagers, the Internet is as much of a daily
life's necessity as food and water. (Maybe more since bathing
is sometimes shaky.) Most teens can be found online several
hours a day, reading entertainment gossip, looking at pornography—and some "weirdos" even use it for schoolwork!
Teens actively socialize with the peers they know and thousands of people they'll never know, from all corners of the
world on websites like MySpace and Facebook. The capa-
bilities range from fantastic to frightening. Teenagers can
apply to Ivy League colleges online—and with a credit card,
also buy prescription drugs. The only regulatory body that
stands between your teenager and Internet access is actually
you. As if you don't already have enough to do, feel free to
polish up that Internet Police badge. You're gonna be flash-
ing it.

"This country is a democracy.
But this house is a dictatorship."

—Bridget, mother of four

Your kids likely don't remember life pre-PC, which means you're playing in their world now. They are *way* more savvy here than you could ever be. They know how to block information, hide their websites, and use a hundred different screen names. The real brains can easily undo privacy settings and block software designed to track their online movements. (Hint: these are the ones who should be applying online to Ivy League schools.) If your teen is not one of these, look into the tracking software . . . it's handy-dandy. Otherwise accept the fact that you cannot beat them at their own game. Instead of fighting them on this one, try joining them. As horrifying as that may sound, it actually has its benefits.

The most important benefit is that a shrewd parent can actually use the Internet to get to know her kid better. Almost nothing else in today's world will give you a better sense of what your child's public persona is and what your teen is really doing than getting an inner look at your teen-agers' Facebook or MySpace page. If you dare.

The key to cracking this inner sanctum is monitoring the monitor. This means that if you want to stand a chance at policing Internet usage, you can't allow your teenagers to hide in their bedrooms with the laptop. Physical access is extremely important, because public viewing is the greatest deterrent to keeping teens off unacceptable websites. Make the choice to place the family computer in an easily acces-sible location. Pick a place adults pass by consistently and can easily glance over the shoulder of distracted teenagers before they can hide the page. Also, use the element of sur-prise and at a relaxed moment, ask your teenager to see his/her page. Once on, also ask to check out some of their links and some of their friends' profiles. If they resist, it's probably safe to say that they have something to hide. If so, reach over and turn off the computer, just like that. Boom. Then above their plaintive wails just tell them you'll discuss it the next day, because today they are clearly not capable of handling their computer privileges.

Once everyone has cooled down, sit down with your teen, go to their MySpace, and explain to them in detail the things you find troubling. These things might include specifics such as where your teen attends school and likes to hang out in their spare time. This seems like benign info to a teenager, but still is potentially dangerous in the online world. Just explain that there are a lot of crazy people in the world, and that while you want MySpace to be fun for them, it's always "safety first."

But if your teen balks at your involvement, or suggestions, don't be afraid to "ground them" from their recreational computer time. Remember your teenager has no civil liberties or rights to computer access, and although they may threaten, parents cannot be reported to Child Protective Services for denying computer usage. Sure you'll have one incredibly pissed off teenager, but what else is new? It won't be the first or last time that will happen. You've heard police work is thankless, and you know parenthood is too. This is what happens when the twain shall meet.

Monitoring the Monitor, Part 2: TV & Video Games

"Virtual reality." Isn't that kinda like "jumbo shrimp?" No matter. Television and video games can be a perfectly fine way to escape the stress and pressures of teenage life—if used safely and sparingly. And everybody knows how teens like to use things safely and sparingly.

Controlling the TV used to be simple: Dad had the remote, as nature intended, and that was pretty much that. But with the invention of the DVD and DVR (not to mention the fact that the average American household has more than two television sets), teenagers can now easily schedule TV and movie viewing for convenient (read, when Dad is not around) times and video games are readily available via your home entertainment system or online. Not so simple anymore, eh?

While teenagers do need downtime to "chill out" and relax, discourage the early warning signs of couch potatoism. Encourage them to play sports, join a club, get a part-time job, or socialize with their friends (the ones you like, anyway). Even video games like the Wii make players get up and move around and that's a big plus. No one is suggesting that the TV is evil; at best it can be informative and (with a few exceptions) at worst it is simply a harmless way of unwinding and passing time. But teenagers should use television and video games as an escape from life, not an alternative to life.

Cell Phone Culture

Unfortunately, when your teen is not on the computer, watching TV, or playing video games, she is talking or texting on her cell phone.

While we give our teens (and sometimes preteens) cell phones ostensibly so "we can always find them," there is a backlash. They actually use the darn things! And not just to talk. Text messaging is even bigger, and now many phones provide Internet access as well. Phones are now hand-held computers and are priced accordingly. They also apparently have the power to create teen sociopathia, as evidenced by the fact that teens are utterly shameless about when and where they will use them. (Anytime, anyplace.)

Ponder this teen conversation—held on cell phones, of course . . .

Jessica: Oh my God, really? They grounded you for talking on the phone *they* gave you? Hello, that's what it's *for*!

Melissa: I know, right?

Jessica: That is so wrong. How many minutes last month?

Melissa: Like six thousand.

Jessica: Is that a lot?

Melissa: My dad is like Mr. Math. He says it's more than three hours a day every day.

Jessica: Aren't there like twenty hours in a day? Three is like nothing! That leaves a lot more.

Melissa: I know, right? Like excuse me for having friends.

Jessica: What do they want you to do instead, just IM all day?

Melissa: No, worse. Do homework, clean my room, and be a member of the family, if you can believe it.

Jessica: They actually said that?

Melissa: They like actually said that.

Jessica: No way. That's like . . . child abuse.

Melissa: I know, right?

The conversation would have gone on longer, but Melissa had to hang up so she could text message this traumatic tale to Elisa. And Jenna. And Amanda. And so on.

In theory, your teen having a cell phone is a good idea. Other good theories that haven't turned out so well include Communism, hot pants, and that whole "the world is flat" thing. The trick, of course, is to keep things under control, at least kindasorta. Your best bet is to have your teen on a family cell plan where you can monitor their minutes. Make sure text messaging is included or else you run the risk of being accused of child abuse. How much is too much? If you don't recognize your teen unless they are holding a cell phone to their ear, that's too much. If they are talking on their cell and put their hand down and the phone stays there on its own, that's too much. If the skin of the ear actually grows around the phone, that's too much. And the idea of teens talking/texting while driving . . . yikes. Let's not even go there.

The Clash of the Curfew

There was a time when "Keeping up with the Joneses" was reserved for suburban yuppies. (This was before the word "yuppies" actually existed, although the yuppies themselves have been around awhile. Not that there's anything wrong with them.) This usually included a nice green manicured lawn, a shiny new car or two in the driveway, and maybe even a grinning lawn jockey holding a lantern in the front yard. Your teens will want those things too, except of course the TeenTown version (so you can 86 the lawn jockey). Yes, your teens will want what their peers/friends have—or more. Probably more. And yes, they will want all the right "stuff." But at this age they also want something you can't buy at a mall. They want freedom. Particularly at night. So now we're talking curfew.

For many teens, curfew = adulthood; the less they have of the former, the more they have of the latter. Adults self-create curfews based upon common sense, their A.M. responsibilities, and simply how late they can stay awake. Teens wouldn't let any of these mere details stand in their way of staying out all night. Or all week. Or all month. So what are they doing out there somewhere so late, anyway? Mostly, they're just getting away from you. Let them. But not too much.

Remembering that this is ultimately All About You, realize that their curfew is really **your** curfew. If you can't stay up past 11, guess what time they need to be home? Most parents can't sleep until everyone is back home and the house is locked down for the night. You might have to extend yourself slightly on the weekends, but that's why God created coffee. Curfews should start early and gradually increase with age, sort of like an allowance. Tell your teen that they will get as much responsibility as they can handle and they'll get the chance to prove it. This creates a cause-and-effect scenario that is more about their reliability and maturity and less about your "pathetically out of touch beyond-ancient parentosity," such as when you hand them a $5 bill and tell them to go have fun.

When establishing a curfew, find out where exactly your teen will be and what they will be doing. If there are specific, reasonable plans with set times involved (like a movie or a school dance), try to be a little flexible so your teen doesn't have to leave anything early. (Since, Ohmigod, that would be soooooooo embarrassing!) But if they are just "hanging out," then they can just as easily (though not as happily) hang out at home after 10. That's a good starting point for a teen on weekends and vacations. As they get older, increase to 11 and eventually 12. The truth is there is no reason for any teenager to be out after 1 A.M., ever. The world can be a dangerous place, and it's much more dangerous late at night. "The bars don't close till two" should not be considered a valid reason to extend this, and in fact might even be cause for Curfew Regression.

Curfew Regression

Curfew regression is really just a grown-up name for a time-out that should occur when a curfew is missed. Don't make a big deal about it, don't ground them (unless they broke other rules such as drinking alcohol), just simply point out that they missed their curfew, so they're not ready for the later time and you'll be going back to the previous curfew for awhile until they can re-establish it again. They'll hate that . . . but they will also see that it was created by their own actions, and the punishment definitely fits the crime.

One caveat: if for some reason your teen is going to be late, calling you before curfew is a must. And don't sweat them being a few minutes late. The last thing you need is some teenager speeding home to make curfew. If they are a few minutes late, point it out and suggest they leave a little earlier next time. Mercy is never a bad thing, especially as they find their way and you believe they are making a legitimate effort. But if they try to play you, and treat you like a graduate of the University of Stupid, come down on them and come down on them hard. And if they're soooooooooo embarrassed, that's just soooooooooo too bad.

Every Parent's Worst Nightmare: The Driver's License!

Woe is you. That's where this is going, so let's just start there. Time to get your self-pity on. You birthed them, you wiped their dirty butts, you blew their snotty noses, you cleaned their pukey puke. You bought them nice clothes they wouldn't wear, good food they wouldn't eat, and expensive toys they wouldn't play with. And now this. These are the thanks you get. Life is, say it out loud, so unfair.

Sure, they're dabbling with uglier things: the sex stuff, the drugs stuff, the alcohol stuff. The overly dramatic diaries of how their adolescence is the hardest adolescence in the history of adolescenci. But at least they have the human decency to keep those things secret from you. This is different. This time, you will actually be their partner in crime. Or at the very least, an unindicted co-conspiritor. Getting his driver's license is your child's most clear-cut act of independence since you dropped him off for the first day of school a decade ago. They're all ready to go "on the grid" for the first time and take on official, legal, adult responsibilities. The literal and figurative big separation. They're ready to be on their own . . . as long as they get mommy and daddy's help. Oh, the irony.

This section is a "how-to." Not a "how-to" get your teenager a driver's license, but "how-to" simply survive the experience. Because as we know, as scary letters go, right up there with "IRS" are "DMV." If you are already into this process, you don't need to be told how this sucks for you. You already know.

First off, it's vital that you don't show fear. Like dogs, teens can smell fear. And if yours (teen that is) gets even a whiff of the sheer terror you have going on inside—which is totally, completely, and absolutely legit by the way—it'll make everything that much worse. Not that it could really get much worse, to be honest.

"A driver's license is a freedom license.

With a really bad picture on it."

—Adam, 17

Secondly, let your teen, for lack of a better word, "drive" this process. They tend to fall into one of two camps. The first is the "I want my permit and license so badly I have to get it on the first day possible" camp. These teens will hit the *Driver's Handbook* the way you wish they would attack their geometry text. (Ain't gonna happen.) The other is the "Eh, I don't know . . ." camp. These teens aren't indecisive. They're afraid. While it's theoretically important (yet oh-so-difficult) to listen to your teen in general, really make an effort here. Since we all grow at our own rate, the last thing you want to do is push a teenager behind the wheel of a car if they don't believe they're ready. (The second-to-last thing might be allowing them behind the wheel even if they say they *are* ready, but that's your baggage and you have to get over it pretty much now. Either that or just drive them everywhere, forever.)

If your teen wants to go forward, yes, take them to the DMV and help them get their permit. Then figure out who's going to teach them to drive. A professional driving school is better for them but more importantly *much* better for you. If there is an available adult with the patience of Job, that can work too. If that's you, fine. If it's not, so much the better. Once your teen has a permit, they will ask to drive with you. Say yes. Take them to a big empty parking lot and let them drive around. Gently offer some tips, but refrain from slamming down on the invisible brake, grabbing the steering wheel, or screaming *"Watch out!"* Driving is about concentration and confidence and these acts inspire neither and just make you look bad—worse than their driving could ever be.

Realize a few things going in:

- Your teen's car insurance will be expensive;
- Everyone who drives will hit something eventually;
- Your teen's car insurance will be even more expensive as soon as they hit something.

Take solace in the fact that you're not really spending *your* money anyway. You're spending theirs. Think about it this way: the more of it they spend now, the less you'll be leaving them in your will. It all comes out in the wash.

Don't become frustrated or angry at fender-benders. You'll only get more stressed out and you'll splatter your stress onto your teen as well. Remember that a stressed driver is not a better driver. Just stick to the basics: be sure they're driving a safe vehicle, use seat belts, and are properly insured.

As usual, a conversation is in order. Explain why speeding is a no-no (and if you've forgotten, it's because it cuts down on reaction time and leads to more accidents) and teach them to be considerate to other drivers and how to drive defensively. Many parents put their teens on "cell phone probation" while driving to minimize distractions. Even if you don't, be sure you and your teen know your local laws on "spieling while wheeling"—they vary.

Once licensed, there's nothing left for you to do but hand over the car keys, say "Be careful," lay down the rules about no cell phones or drinking (more about no drinking and driving in Chapter 8), endure the inevitable eye-roll, and watch them drive away in charge of that giant hunk of metal capable of traveling at dangerously high speeds. Although, you do reserve the right to make fun of their driver's license photo, pretty much every single day. Feel free. You've earned it.

School Daze: How to Get Your Kids to Focus on School

The last thing teenagers want is to get the third-degree about school. (Okay, the last thing they want is a tie between a zit on prom night and being seen in public with their parents. But this is the next-to-last thing they want.) Nobody wants to be plagued with "Did you do your homework?" or "What did you get on that math test?" or "See that guy picking up trash on the highway, he failed biology too!"

So how to be supportive and encouraging but still make sure those lazy attitude-challenged slobs do what they're supposed to do in school? As usual, it won't be easy since the rubber hose thing is still against the law. Every teen, regardless of aptitude, will face some academic challenges along the way, whether it's subjects they just don't "get" or problems with specific teachers who don't see the same brilliance in your child that you do.

Focus and structure are good places to start. Make sure they have a routine (regularly settling down to homework either after school or after dinner) and a clean, organized, quiet space in which to work. Let them choose a place (within reason) that suits them: the desk in their room, the kitchen table, on the floor in the living room, and so on. The location doesn't matter as long as they can get their work done. And no, they can't get their work done during the party at Kelsey's, or in the car on the way to Todd's, or while sitting on the bench during their soccer game. Don't leave it to them, but keep in mind that teenagers are much more likely to stick with a homework routine if they are the one to set it up. Just make sure it makes sense.

Since most teens would rather be having fun than doing homework (some would prefer dental surgery actually), it's up to you to minimize their distractions. No TV, No iPod, No instant messaging, No e-mail during homework time. There is no multitasking during homework time. There is only tasking, AKA homework.

All students are not created equal. Well maybe they were created that way, but they don't stay that way for long. They start to separate the day they start receiving grades. You know the drill: some kids will bring home good grades without much prodding from parents (or apparent effort), while others will work hard but struggle academically. And the rest will be up-and-down average students. As your teenager grows up and moves into the big bad world, remember not to overrate the importance of their "permanent record." That exists right alongside Atlantis, Shangri-La, and the Land of Oz. If your teenager is not a high-achieving student, don't stress out. It's not your fault, or your problem, and while grades do measure how much geometry your teen knows or whether they have accurately memorized the periodic table of elements, school grades are neither a measure of a person's self-worth nor an accurate indicator of life success. But don't tell them that or they'll slack off in a class in which they could get an "A."

If you have a teenager who struggles in school, you can help them by launching a pre-emptive strike. During the early weeks of the school year, call or schedule a meeting with their teacher or teachers. Express your desire to stay on top of what your teenager is doing in class, and encourage them to contact you if (and when) things go astray. Of course, your teen will be mortified, but this is a winning strategy as it makes teachers more aware of your child in their classroom, and also sends a strong message to teacher and teen alike that you care about education.

In truth, your teen's teacher is their first outside-the-home "boss." This is a good time to get your teen trained regarding "boss management." If your teen has a problem with a teacher, be careful about too overtly taking your teen's side or undermining the teacher to your teen. It doesn't protect them, it actually takes their power away. Supervise things, but let your teen and the teacher work out any issues themselves. Teachers often have excellent ideas to help get your teenager back on track. And that's what you want. Well, that and a tropical vacation. Which you won't be able to afford until they get out of school.

Privacy (AKA Snoop, Dog)

Okay, so if your teens heard the word "snoop" they would most likely think of the rapper formerly known as Snoop Dogg formerly known as Snoop Doggy Dogg formerly known as Calvin Broadus. (Feel free to impress/horrify your teen by knowing his real name.) But parents know that to snoop (AKA snooping) is actually all about making sure your teens are not into things that they shouldn't be into. Protecting them from their worst enemy—themselves. Snooping is both your right and your responsibility but if you don't do it the right way you'll be causing as many—or potentially more—problems than you are solving. But there are trust issues here, and this time you want to be sure your teen doesn't stop trusting you.

"It's not snooping. It's parenting."

—Jen, mother of two

First off, understand that snooping makes you a P.I. (Parental Investigator) and the P.I. business is not pretty. Most parents will discover things about their teens that they just really didn't want to know. These can range from evidence of sexual activity to drug and alcohol use to animal sacrifice. Okay, probably not animal sacrifice. But you get the idea. Your teens are not kids anymore, they're transitioning into adulthood, and that means transitioning into adult areas which of course you don't want them transitioning into. But this is where you need to start transitioning into dealing with their transitioning.

You have good reason to be concerned. Monitoring teens used to be a lot simpler back in The Proverbial Day. The house used to have three telephones, one in the kitchen, one in the parents' bedroom, and one in the living room or den. All phone conversations were held on one of them, and eavesdropping was not exactly rocket science. With the advent of the cell phone and home computer, though, things have changed forever. The world has become simultaneously smaller and bigger. When you were growing up, your parents knew your friends and probably your friends' parents too. The computer has enlarged neighborhoods. Teens no longer spend their Saturdays with the other kids on the street. Their friends may very well be strangers to you, since they live across town. Your teens don't just meet people at school or sports anymore—they meet them online now, and so say bye-bye to controlling who they know.

So think of this as a "Santa Claus" situation. You are working your kids, to be sure, but it's because you love them and you want them to be safe. This generation of parents are a hybrid—they often want to be half-parent and half-friend and trust their kids. Do them a favor—**don't!** By all means, dig around through their stuff when they're not home. Just don't let them know you're doing it. If you find nothing, all is well. And if you find something, at least you can do something about it, and then all will be well again.

CHAPTER 6

relationships between drama queens & kings

If there's one thing softer than a teenager's head, it's a teenager's heart. In fact, puberty is nature's warning sign of **"Trouble Ahead—Proceed with Caution."** Of course the word "caution" does not appear in the TeenSpeak-English dictionary. So fasten your seatbelts, it's going to be a bumpy night. Year. Decade.

Kids instinctively grow up loving their parents. This love extends to other family members as well, even if they don't like the way Aunt Rhonda smells or the fact that Sissy steals their toys. When they're small, kids make "friends" on a short-term basis with kids their own age who share their most basic activities. But once puberty kicks in, these tweens and newbie teens start meeting peers here, there, and everywhere, and beyond your formerly watchful eye. Oh, they still make friends . . . but now that hormones have set in, they start to make *friends*. These can be platonic *friends* or romantic *friends*, but the bottom line is the same. Fueled by these hormones, there are emotional bonds being created (real or imagined, likely a combination of both, but of course they feel the same). The stakes are raised, and of course as Newton showed us, what goes up must come down. What Sir Isaac failed to postulate was that what goes up for them, comes down on you. So strap on a helmet and let's see if you can't make it through this bumpy night without any further head trauma.

When Their Friendships Just Don't "Clique"

Everything you need to know about high school cliques can be learned from the 1980s movie *The Breakfast Club*. The film featured five students characteristic of stereotypical high school cliques: the popular girl, the jock, the geeky nerd, the weirdo/outcast, and the stoner/loser/thug guy, also known as The One Most Likely to Eventually Become Your Son-In-Law. Although it's impossible to keep up with the ever-changing descriptive jargon, some of the cliques at your teenager's school will certainly include the following stereotypes: Punks, Nerds, Jocks, Druggies, Preps, and Losers. Oh, and of course The Popular Crowd. Other cliques may be known around school as "the benchies" or "the tree peeps." These bizarre clique names come from the various on-campus locations certain groups congregate, and unless your teen is a "benchie" or "tree peep" they'd be wise to park their adolescent asses someplace else. So, if you have managed to repress this political nightmare, rent *The Breakfast Club* for a quickie refresher course. Or better yet, watch it with your teenager.

From vicious "Mommy & Me" playgroups to the highest levels (yet less vicious) of government, cliques exist. Some flourish on inclusion, most thrive on exclusion, but all cliques create a shortcut through humanity in order to sort and classify human beings. Think back to your middle school or high school days and try not to wince. (Nice try.) Most parents can recall the smug satisfaction of being accepted by the crowd or the searing agony of being left out. Coping with cliques is a tough road to navigate because teenagers, well, suck, and your teen's best friend today can be their worst enemy tomorrow, and then back again by Friday, without anyone really knowing why or even remembering that it happened.

This is not to suggest that all cliques are bad. Teenagers do need a sense of belonging to a peer group and many teenagers create cliques not for the purpose of exclusivity, but to find others with whom they feel a connection. And cliques are informal, which allows them to avoid the stigma of The Taxidermy Club.

If your teenager is on the inside of the clique looking in, your problem is—actually you don't have a problem, do you? It's good to be with the "in" crowd. You should regularly remind kids how fleeting popularity can be, and always encourage them to be nice—or at least not taunt or torture—their classmates who may not be so lucky when it comes to social class.

If your teen is on the outside of a clique looking in, the best way to deal with this sort of exclusionary behavior is to help them understand that being "in" isn't everything, and that the kids that promote ostracism do so out of their own low self-esteem or the need to fit in with their group. Yes, you're shining them on, but isn't that your role?

Rejection by a clique is painful and not easy to cope with and there may be tears. But once they've recovered and dried their eyes, encourage your teens to express their frustration and anger when they are rebuffed by a group of peers. Voodoo dolls might be a nice touch here. Churches and temples offer teen groups that will take anybody, as will social causes and charity organizations such as Habitat for Humanity. But let's not be hasty in overlooking those voodoo dolls. If your teen is actually being mistreated by his or her classmates, you have the responsibility to speak to someone at your teen's school about it. Yes, your teen may hate you, but hey—he probably does already. And no kid deserves to feel unsafe or threatened at school or anywhere else.

Sadly, rejection is a part of life and learning to deal with disappointment and pretend you never cared anyway is a part of growing up. Mean girls turn into mean women and bullies don't disappear after high school. Take a quick look around your office staff, your PTA, or your local senior citizens' center and guess what? Underneath the name tags and blue hair you'll find a former jock, popular girl, weirdo, geek, and druggie (your future son-in-law).

The Truth Hurts (So Teens Lie Instead)

Parenting teenagers is tough enough even when everything's on the up-and-up. But these adolescent scoundrels are about to throw a wrench into things. And face it, when wrenches are thrown, by anyone under any circumstances, no good can come of it.

Teenagers lie. They just do. (Yes, even yours. And if they tell you otherwise, they're, well, lying.) They lie to you about their friends, they lie to their friends about you, and they lie to both you and their friends about whether or not they are lying to both you and their friends. It's not enough that you have to be Wolfgang Puck to keep them fed and Calvin Klein to keep them clothed, now you have to be Sherlock Holmes to figure out whodunit, who's doing it, and who needs a good grounding because it was done.

Why Lie?

The #1 reason young children lie is to stay out of trouble. The #1 reason adults lie is to get something they want. The #1 reason teenagers lie is to combat insecurity. Transition and change are difficult for everyone, and if you think about it, adolescence is pretty much six straight years of transition and change. That's a lot of newness and accompanying stress. Imagine starting a new job every year for six years. Or moving every year for six years. Or getting married every year for six years. Or having a baby every year for six years. You'd be on more meds than Dr. Nick prescribed for Elvis.

And since teens are totally preoccupied with themselves, and because in TeenTown there are no molehills, only mountains, odds are they are going to find a lot of fault in that mirror. Their skin is out of control, their hair is out of control, their bodies are out of control, and all they want to do is eat, sleep, and text message, all to excess, because *they* are out of control.

So. They need to regain control. If the real world isn't what they want it to be, then goshdarn it they'll create one that is. Cue the lies.

They'll lie to their friends to make themselves sound more interesting ("I saw a UFO!"), or to gain sympathy ("I may have a fatal disease!"), or to gain respect ("I got 20,000 on my SAT's!"). Those lies won't work on you because you know better. But remember that they are telling these lies to other teens, who are telling their own lies right back, so nobody is calling anybody out on anything lest they in turn be called out themselves. Isn't it simpler to be a grownup? Even though you have to go to work and pay taxes and endure the DMV, aren't you like way ahead for the most part?

The lies at home will be fewer, because there's a better chance you could bust them. But these lies will most likely be regarding something more important than UFOs. And they won't be of the "insecurity" nature either. They will be a balance of the kid lies (to avoid getting into trouble) and the adult lies (to get something they want).

This is fitting since teens are firmly between childhood and adulthood. So be careful of the old I'm-sleeping-over-at-Jessica's-while-Jessica's-parents-are-being-told-she's-sleeping-at-your-house trick. They still try that one, just like you did when you were a teen, and it sometimes still works.

But keep things clear: "You cannot lie to me. It's not okay. And that's the truth." Make it clear to them that in the long run, telling the truth—even when confessing a major mess-up—will pay off much better than you catching them in a lie.

Betrayal

For teenagers, loyalty is a murky concept. But, betrayal they get. Maybe this is because teens must hold themselves accountable for loyalty, and yet get to place the blame for betrayal on others. It's a neat little teen trick which falls under the all-encompassing heading of "It's Not My Fault."

Every day, betrayal runs rampant through middle and high school hallways. Lifelong friendships come apart over broken promises and secrets exposed. Ugly gossip and rumors are posted for the masses over the Internet. Boys and girls both struggle with the "BFF" (Best Friends Forever, duh) concept which only wreaks havoc with creating and maintaining friendships. Your teen may be semi-happily conjugating verbs in Spanish class, while down the hall in AP chemistry, gossip and rumors are burying them big-time. The wounds they believe they are suffering are not really big things, they just feel like them to your teenager, and thus—Dramalicious.

Dramalicious

Tune in for the latest episode of *As the Teenage World Turns*. Most of the time, teen betrayal feels very much like a soap opera. A bad soap opera. A really bad soap opera.

Emily is seventeen and has no car. Her BFF Melissa, who does, agrees to drive her to The Big Party. Melissa has driven Emily everywhere for months without complaint. But at the last minute, Melissa's mother has car problems, needs to borrow Melissa's car, and can't return it to her until just before the party starts. Because they live on opposite sides of the city, this means Melissa can't drive Emily to the party. Melissa feels bad. Emily feels betrayed. Emily's next move is to call everyone she knows to tell them of Melissa's treachery. How *could* she? Dramalicious! Emily used a hundred tissues and would have clunked Melissa over the head with the empty box if she'd had the chance.

When Nick's girlfriend Michelle put a picture of herself (although an innocent one) on her Facebook page with another guy in it, Nick went ballistic and there was an ugly public scene in the school cafeteria. Dramalicious! Bring on the tissues for the crying! And the empty box for the hitting!

When occasions like these erupt with your teen, your best bet is to run off to your summer house even if it's winter. If you don't have a summer house, get one fast. If that's not possible, and you have to be there, try to help your teen get their perspective on the situation. But first let them "punch/cry themselves out"; they're easier to deal with when weakened.

In Emily's case, it was fine to be upset about the change in plans, but she had time to still make the party and yes she had to bribe her sister with a sushi lunch to get a ride but really what damage was done? Emily just needed to chill out and realize that Melissa has been a great friend to her and nobody's perfect and sometimes we have to cut our friends some slack. But sometimes teens would rather just have a pity party because it's (you got it) Dramalicious! In Nick's case, he should have confronted Michelle privately about his concerns. Their issue was actually a smaller problem than the way it was handled. Two days after their blow-up they were back together, but for weeks received smirks in the halls from everyone treated to their public argument.

However, sometimes more serious issues of betrayal do occur over and above standard Dramaliciousness, which do become a parental problem. (This is where you come in.)

Teen Drama: The Real Thing

After a sleepover with some girlfriends, Erica, age fourteen, was horrified to find out that one of them had snapped her picture with a cell phone camera while she was in the shower and had e-mailed it to some other girls with a note attached: "Check out these boobs—fake or real?" Of course, the prank didn't end there. The unwelcome cell phone photo traveled from computer to computer, across town, across state lines, and eventually onto a teenage porn website.

Colton, fifteen, was the victim of a rumor that he was gay after he was spotted comforting a male friend whose father has just been diagnosed with cancer. Rumors were passed around school for weeks, hurting both boys immensely. In order to protect themselves, these boys who had been friends since first grade, avoided each other like the plague.

In these more difficult examples, these teens are not soap opera characters creating drama but real victims of social exploitation by peers and they need to count on the adults in their lives for assistance, defense, and support. When your teenager comes to you complaining of injustice and torment, it's up to you to decide whether the betrayal is worthy of ignoring it, or talking to other adults whose teens are involved in order to put out the fire.

With Friends Like Those, You Need a Bottle of Scotch

Odds are they won't show up wearing a black hat, or sporting an evil laugh, or with the words "Bad News" tattooed across their foreheads. If only it were so simple. But the chances of your teen avoiding some bad seeds are about as good as Britney Spears putting a Mother of the Year Award on her mantel in the near future.

They say opposites attract and when it comes to teens, they're right. People are always curious about those different from them. If you are raising your teens in a secure and steady home, it's because you have expectations, rules, and boundaries. Which are teens' favorite things, right above cleaning their rooms, Brussels sprouts, and reruns of *Masterpiece The-atre.* As a result, your teen would experience one of those "the grass is always greener" situations by making a friend whose home life consists of doing whatever they want pretty much whenever they want. Although perhaps you can't conceive of it yourself, these situations actually do exist, usually due to literal or figurative parental absence.

You really can't blame your teen for wanting less supervision and rules. But be prepared. Once they get a taste of the fantasy adult life at their "other house"—that is, more freedom, less responsibility—your place will seem even more strict. So some acting out should be expected.

But where this situation could become dangerous isn't when your teen is back with you—it's when they are at their "other" house, unsupervised. Since teens (fueled by hormones and without much life experience) tend to feel immortal anyway, when coupled with a lack of parental supervision the results can be tragic. In a related issue, your teen's new friend may be happy for their freedom on the surface, but down deep resent the indifference of their parents. This may cause them to "act out" via risky behavior as an attention-getting device. These self-abusive activities could be related to drugs, alcohol, sex, or an attempt to buck authority (e.g., committing crimes or thrillseeking in ways like street racing). Don't be fooled into believing your teen "is too smart" to get caught up in these sorts of things. Because they're not. They're really not.

There are other ways your teen can be "Svengali'd." Be cautious if they start to spend time with someone who is older or more popular. An older friend may be emotionally ready for experiences your teen is not—and your teen may find herself in over her head as a result. Having a more popular friend might provide an ego boost to your teen, but might also create some sort of pressure (real or imagined) to be "worthy" of a step up in social class . . . which could result in feeling a need to prove himself.

"When I was a sophomore this group of seniors let me hang out with them and I thought I was so cool. Then one night they broke into a house and I was with them and we got caught and into huge trouble. That wasn't cool at all."

—Jake, 17

If your teen starts to change after "chillin'" with their new friend, and you don't like the changes you're seeing, then it's time to put the chill on the "chillin'." If possible, get the new friend into your house and size him up yourself. Ask questions. It's really the only chance you have to figure out whether your teen could be coming under a bad influence. If necessary, that can lead to "a talk" with your teen about how you don't approve of his friend, and why. If you have probable cause—"not liking their looks" is *not* probable cause—then maybe it's time they saw a bit less of one another, or they only hang out at your house, when you're home, so you can keep tabs on things.

It's all so much more complicated now. Oh, for the days of yore when Eddie Haskells were Eddie Haskells, and the Cleavers weren't fooled for a minute.

"Going Out with Someone"— ## What It Means Through the Ages

Remember the 1950s? Of course you don't, because either you weren't alive then, or you were but were too young to recall them, or you're just so old now that you can't remember what you wore yesterday, much less the 1950s. But back in the 1950s there was a high school senior named Teddy (in the 1950s there actually were boys named Teddy), who asked his sophomore classmate Jane (in the 1950s there actually were girls named Jane) to "Go Steady." She giggled about it with her girlfriends and wore his letterman jacket and class ring as a sign of their "oneness."

Remember the 1980s? Of course you don't, because either you were doing things in the 1980s that makes it difficult to remember things, or just because the 1980s were so ridiculous you simply choose not to. But back in the 1980s a boy named Adam asked his classmate Jennifer if she would "Go" with him while four of her girlfriends were secretly listening in on the extension phones. "Go" was the fuzzy math version of coupling up and often garnered the confused response of "Go where?" After the giggling on the extension phones subsided, with a detailed explanation that "Go" meant not actually going anywhere but simply "be a couple," Adam and Jennifer's three-week long courtship then culminated in a kiss at the seventh-grade dance.

Today, the "going steady" idea has morphed into something so common that preteens as young as fifth graders are playing fast and loose with the concept as their earliest introduction to dating. To have your preteen announce over a Happy Meal at the playground that they are "going out with someone" can be a bit of a shocker, but don't panic. No need to call around for convent vacancies or book that Oprah appearance, because in modern-day parlance "going out with someone" actually means "staying in, alone."

To young teens, "going out" means finding out from your friends that someone "likes you." If you in turn "like them back," it's pretty much a done deal. The middle school grapevine spreads the word—they're a couple. They're "going out."

But these days "going out" doesn't lend itself to heavy petting under the jungle gym or long hours snuggled in a booth together at the local Chuck E. Cheese. In this pre-driving world of conflicting schedules and busy parents, proximity-challenged youngsters discover that "going out" is far easier than "getting together."

Instead, this relationship will exist mostly via technology: the house phone, personal communication device text messaging, instant message computer chats, MySpace postings and photos, e-mails, and of course the trusty cell phone, which is especially convenient during normal household sleeping hours and on-the-run emergencies, like calling to broadcast every detail such as, "I'm going to 7-Eleven after baseball practice, so I might be out of communication for over an hour." (This type of consideration and communication disappears immediately upon marriage, which, coincidentally, also sucks.)

True, a particularly adventurous preteen or young teen may attempt to set up an actual face-to-face date with their beloved after spending hours discussing with friends just when and how the "going out" couple will share their first kiss, but rest assured it's really big talk and no action. Max's skateboard is simply not a reliable mode of transportation for two and Layla's braces just got tightened at the orthodontist, so these attempts to rendezvous will be easily thwarted in favor of e-mailing and calling each other endlessly—oh, and of course, keeping the involved friends informed of any and all late-breaking news. Not that there really is any.

"Going Out" is generally the fantasy role-play of young teens preparing themselves for the next stage of teen court-ship and dating. Welcome to the world of "Hooking Up."

Hope you didn't lose the numbers for that convent and the Oprah show. Because now you're going to need them.

Chaperoning Your Dating Teen

No surprise: parenting has tradeoffs. You get to declare them as tax deductions, they give you birthday gifts, and once in awhile they say something really funny. In exchange you have to put up with a lot of crap. But as you have probably concluded by now, parenthood has one of the worst Pain-to-Gain ratios in the history of Pain-to-Gain ratios.

When it comes to chaperoning your dating teen, there are two distinct methods, Direct and Indirect. The Direct (hands-on) approach applies to younger teens, while the Indirect (hands-off) is for older teens. Both are tricky, and neither are fun, but both must be done.

Direct Chaperoning

When your teens start dating, it won't really be dating. It will be multiple kids going to a movie. Easy. But eventually it will get to be one-on-one and you'll be called upon to provide transportation services. That of course is all your teen will want you to provide. (Well that and the money for the movie. And the pizza after. And the ice cream after that. Their dates will cost you $50 and you won't even see the movie or eat the ice cream or pizza. This parenthood thing is just bogus. At the end of the day the tax deductions and birthday gifts don't begin to offset the bogusity, although when they say something funny sometimes it's really funny so that does help.)

"We try to be flexible about our daughter Ashley's social life. We have only one non-negotiable rule. If a boy takes her out on a date, he needs to come to the house, get out of his car, ring the doorbell, come inside, and make small talk with my wife or me first. If he won't do that, he doesn't really want to date Ashley. And he's not going to."

—Steve

Younger teens are really too young to simply drop off and leave there. (That's not chaperoning. That's just driving.) So there may be a couple of awkward years here where Mom and/or Dad have to accompany their children on dates. Expect your teen's appreciation for this to be about as enthusiastic as if you invited them to dinner at The House of Soy. Part of dating in the first place is about getting away from your stinking parents, and of course you have no intention of making that happen at their age. (To be fair, at least for a moment, imagine how you would feel if they were coming along on your dates.)

So now it's about creating the proper choreography. How do you give them the illusion of independence while at the same time tailing them like a P.I. so you can spy on their every move? Well if the plan is a movie, that's easy. If it's a multiplex (and they pretty much all are) you can either find a movie you want to see at approximately the same time (if you're the semi-trusting type) or you can go to the same movie as the little Romeo and Juliet (if you're not). If it's lunch or dinner, same deal. You all go, sit at separate tables, and enjoy. However if they're doing something less structured (especially if it involves them being someplace in motion) you'll need to be creative. So if you haven't installed a microchip into them so far, this might be a good time.

Indirect Chaperoning

Indirect Chaperoning comes later. Just because you are no longer wanted or needed to dust off the chauffeur's cap doesn't mean you just let them head off to who-knows-where to do who-knows-what with who-knows-who. Train your teen to have the standard info ready in advance—who are they going with, where are they going, what will they be doing, who else will be there, and what time will they be home? Make sure your teen has a charged cell phone and require that they check in with you regularly—maybe once every two hours. Yes, they'll be mortified, but a quick conversation to confirm that they're where they said they're going to be never killed anyone (yet). And if they are going out to eat, make sure they bring you back a doggie bag. You might as well get something out of this.

Breaking Up Is Hard to Do (And Even Harder on You)

Whether it's more like *Romeo and Juliet* or *10 Things I Hate About You*, just about every teenager harbors the fantasy of falling in love and having an adoring, affectionate, and committed connection to another person. Being in love provides your teen with a new best friend and helps to ease the anxieties of much typical teenage insecurity. A teenager in love feels powerful and desired and has someone to share acne cream with. Their self-esteem takes a huge leap. But huge leaps are often followed by loud splats.

"Being in love is the best.

Except when it's the worst."

—Annie, 16

So, what happens when the love songs stop playing, and suddenly the calls and texts go unanswered? Say hello to the dark side of love. It's the breakup. If it was your teen's idea, you've got a chance. But if it wasn't—oy. Your teen will be hurt, angry, frustrated, and embarrassed. Expect them to complain, sleep, and mope about. More than usual, even. Sadly, just when your teen is at their worst—the most unpleasant and the most unlovable—is exactly when they require you to provide them with unconditional parental love. Mostly this means just having mercy on them. More than usual, even. If you're lucky, they'll just disappear into their room, commiserate with friends, write angry e-mails, and play loud music. More than usual, even.

Of course, you could tell them how the euphoria of new love is impossible to sustain and that their broken heart will heal and that someday your teenager will love again. However, do so at your own risk, because although true, these messages will result in them throwing things at you.

Your best bet is to keep your distance until time eventually heals this wound. Maybe knock on their door to offer a snack or make an impromptu trip to a ballgame or just spend some time watching a movie. But be smart—find something other than *Romeo and Juliet*.

CHAPTER 7

sex: from hanging out to hooking up!

Good news! Now we get to the sex stuff! Oh, wait, forgot . . . this book is for the parents. Check that. Rewind. Okay—Bad news! Now we get to the sex stuff! Not that there hasn't been bad news before now. Hmm, okay, so maybe it's better to say now we get to more bad news. (Don't you wish your parents told you that parenthood sucks? That secret really is the Great Parental Revenge . . . and some day it will be yours! All yours! Hahahahahaha!) But for now . . .

Yes, this chapter is about what happens when your teens stop wanting to touch only themselves and start wanting to touch others, who in turn may or may not want to touch your teen back. Kinda creepy thought, huh. Teens think it's disgusting to imagine their parents having sex. But when parents imagine their teens having sex? It's enough to make you lose feeling from the waist down. And from the waist up too, for that matter. In your day, teens thought a lot more about touching than doing it. These days, not so much.

Like tax day, you know this is coming, so you might as well get ready for it. Unlike tax day, you can't circle your calendar to prepare for it. More like circling the wagons once it's upon you. And even if you think it's not upon you yet . . . it just may be . . .

So let's get to the discussion. About "hooking up" (AKA casual sex), dating (AKA auditioning for sex), and of course, sex (AKA aaaahhhh!!!!).

The First Time: A Relatively True Story

Sex and birth control. Which is the chicken and which is the egg? (In this case the "egg" reference might be a pun too far.) Some parents believe that just as sure as they have clothes under their beds, teens will have sex, so it's their job to introduce them to the concept of birth control. Other parents believe that providing birth control info is simply giving teens permission to have sex. Regardless of which camp you fall into, here's a relatively true story of how it came down for one family . . .

Lisa was greeted at the door by her teenage niece, Heidi. Heidi was breathless and giggly and she grabbed Lisa by the arm and said, "Come up to my room and see what Richie gave me." Richie and Heidi had been dating steadily for almost two years. She had just turned sixteen, while he was a few months older.

Once behind closed doors in her bedroom, Heidi opened a dresser drawer and pulled out a pair of leopard print thong underwear. She held them up, beaming. "Nice," said Lisa, wondering where this conversation was going. "Those are very cute." Heidi just grinned like the Cheshire cat. But Lisa, in addition to being the favorite aunt, was also way too nosy to let it just end there. "Heidi, just so you know, no teenage boy gives a teenage girl underwear unless he plans on seeing her wearing them." Heidi didn't miss a beat. "Oh, he's seen me wearing them." Pause. "And not wearing them."

So.

Now that the leopard thong underwear was out of the drawer, the cat was out of the bag. Heidi and Richie had had sex. Lisa remained calm, although she was shocked. (As much as anything, she was shocked that the leopard thong was sexier than anything Lisa owned.) But from Lisa's perspective, Heidi's choice was not unhealthy. Heidi was a good, stable kid in a committed long-term relationship. She and Richie didn't "do it" under the influence of drugs or alcohol. They didn't do it in the bathroom at the mall. It had not been a "cheap" or "ugly" experience. They had both been virgins at the time and had used a condom. Apparently, it hurt a little and Heidi cried, but as she happily told Lisa, "Richie cried too." Also, Lisa was not Heidi's parent. So there was that. Her stake in all this was much less and her perspective slightly different.

Okay, so.

The deed has been done. Now what?

Predictably, Heidi begged Lisa not to tell her parents. Surprisingly, Lisa agreed. Heidi was relieved—for about thirty seconds. That's how long it took Lisa to inform Heidi that Heidi, herself, would be the one to tell them. Predictably, Heidi was horrified. More begging ensued. But Lisa held firm, telling Heidi that if she was old enough to have sex, she was old enough to be honest with her parents about it. Heidi relented, and Lisa offered to be there for the conversation for moral support.

Heidi confided that she felt happy. She felt Richie was a good choice for her first time because he treated her well and she'd never regret it with him. And it had brought them closer together. They were permanently bonded now in a very special way. Lisa was floored by Heidi's maturity. She couldn't help but think about her own less-than-perfect first time and also wondered where the heck Richie found that cute leopard thong and how she could find out without actually asking.

Heidi's mother took the news well. Heidi's father did too under the circumstances. (The "circumstances" being he's a man and Heidi is his daughter, so anything less than "I knew I should have bought that Uzi!" must be considered "taking the news well.") Heidi's mother took Heidi to a gynecologist, who prescribed birth control pills. Heidi's father opted to take up yoga as a stress-reliever rather than go on antidepressants.

Heidi and Richie remained together as a couple throughout high school. Due to their "safe sex" practices, Heidi did not become pregnant or contract an STD or any of that "Movie of the Week" sort of drama. When the time came for them to go off to college, they agreed they would go their separate ways. Several years later, they remain friends and continue to feel positive about their first time together.

So.

While that was a virtually true story, and pleasant enough, what can be learned from it?

Three things:

1. Sex happens whether the parents freak out or not;
2. The healthier the home environment, the better the odds that the situation, though potentially volatile, can be handled with understanding and dignity;
3. Heidi's father doesn't own an Uzi.

If you're unsure of when to have a discussion with your teenager, watch for the tiny clues. Things such as leopard thong underwear, an opened box of condoms, or hotel room charges in Las Vegas might be a good tip-off. Your teenager is expecting you to be shocked and disapproving (which is why they will hide this from you with every ounce of deceit they can beg, borrow, or steal), and you very well may feel that way. However, if you can suppress the urge to scream and yell and ground them for life—and instead simply start a conversation without appearing judgmental—you just might get a teeny, tiny, miniscule opening to have your opinion heard. Plain and simple, if you seem approachable, you are more likely to be approached. Which, whether you realize it or not, is a good thing.

And if it's too much for you to handle, try yoga.

Talking the Talk: The Birds, the Bees, and Beyond

So today's the day. Today's the day you've decided to have The Talk with your teenager. Not the "when mommies and daddies love each other, a baby comes along" talk that you had when they were little. That one was easy, because it was a win-win: you "did the right parental thing" by having it (win #1), plus afterwards your kids still had zero idea what you were talking about (win #2). No, this one will be the real deal, all right, but you're ready. You are ready to channel what your parents told you (most of which turned out to be false), you've read up a little, and besides, you're a modern-day parent. Hey, their friends call you by your first name! You can handle this! They need to know this stuff, so you need to tell them.

"I was afraid that having a real, totally honest conversation with my
teenaged daughter about sex was going to change our relationship
forever. And it did—it actually brought us closer."

—Robin

So all that adds up to a little sit-down with your teen
over hot cocoa and cookies. And it sounds a little something
like this:

You: Now that you're heading off to high school, it
seems like a good time to have a talk.
Your Teen: Is this about sex?
You: Ah, well, yes, actually, it is.
Your Teen: Okay. What do you want to know?

Hmm. Maybe you weren't as ready for this as you thought
you were. Whether it's from viewing an hours-old placenta
brought to science class by Tommy's midwife mother, or
practicing rolling condoms onto bananas in sex education
class, or knowing not only what oral sex is, but actually discussing over pizza in the school cafeteria who's doing it to
whom, teenagers today walk into the talk more educated
than ever before. And maybe more educated than you.
    The children of every generation become sexually aware
and sexually active younger than the previous generation. It
is no longer unusual to find girls and boys as young as twelve
and thirteen who are experimenting with kissing, fondling,
and oral sex. No, this isn't your kid. But of course, that's
what every parent is saying. Some of you are wrong. (But
not you. Oh, no.)

Teenagers are ready for sex physically far sooner than they are ready for sex emotionally. Having sex too soon and/or under the wrong circumstances is not healthy and can lead to longer-term issues. So what can a parent tell them? Well maybe just start with that. It's less about "don't do it" (even though you don't want them to) and more about "try to understand what this is all about."

Teens have sex for many reasons. One is to feel desirable during a time they often don't. Another is that mainstream society tells teens (and all of us) that sex is cool, sex is fun, and being sexy is the ultimate achievement in life. Sex can also be about the shock value, hormonal relief, rebellion, and crossing the line forever between being a kid and being a grownup. Because kids don't have sex, grownups do. That line may still be there, but it's gotten very, very blurry now.

So since your teenager already knows the "facts of life," as well as every dirty little secret about the sex lives of the rich and famous, what does the modern-day sex talk look like? You still have the adult perspective about sex to bring to the table: emotions, responsibility, commitment. (If you don't have a clue about these things, either learn them fast, make something up, or let someone else play the role of "you" during this discussion.)

Some areas to be covered in your talk:

- The only sure-fire way to avoid STDs and unwanted pregnancy is abstinence.
- Despite "new school" thinking, oral sex IS sex, both from an emotional and potential STD perspective.
- Most (but not all) condoms provide reliable protection from STDs, but condoms are one of the least reliable forms of birth control since so many people use them incorrectly.

- The Pill is a reliable form of birth control, but does not protect against STDs.
- Sex changes a relationship. It just does. Sure, it can make it stronger, but in many teenage relationships (and some adult ones too), it can end it too. Use the adage that's been around for generations: boys use love to get sex, girls use sex to get love.

These days the parental role is simple. Make the cocoa, bake the cookies, initiate the conversation, say your piece, and then just sit there. Because nowadays The Talk is mostly The Listen.

Defining Togetherness

Whereas younger teens overstate their sense of commitment to one another, older teens tend to understate. Once upon a time girls yearned for commitment while boys avoided it like taking showers in high school gym class, and through that fundamental incompatibility a balance was achieved in the adolescent universe. But in today's TeenTown the genders have pretty much joined forces in the Zen of "Whatever," which has thrown this symmetry into chaos and will (of course) make your life even more difficult than it is now, even though you don't think that's possible. It so is.

The pursuit of sex for teenagers will always exist, but it can make you insane (which of course presumes you are still sane) trying to keep tabs on the current trends your teenager may be dealing with since the methods and players are ever-changing. The idea that teenage boys are hormonally driven animals constantly on the prowl for sex and that teenage girls spend their days fending them off is becoming a rapidly changing stereotype. Likely fueled by a generation of mothers who have schooled their sons in the art of respecting the female population, teenage boys are actually behaving better than ever. Teenage girls, on the other hand, are a whole different kettle of estrogen. In today's world, if you suggest to your modern teen daughter that she sit home and paint her nails and wait for a potential date to call, be prepared for her to laugh so hard she will snort her Diet Coke through her nose. So grab a paper towel and read on—if you dare.

While that may be hard to grasp, just remember this: boys used to fantasize the way they wanted girls to dress. Nowadays the girls dress that way, voluntarily. Take a look at your kid's school yard and you may confuse the teen girls for cage dancers. Their skirts are short. Their necklines are low. And both their bra straps are g-strings exposed for all to see. That's why you should tell your daughter that when it comes to clothing, less is more (no, not less clothing, but less *provocative* clothing). Tell her that the only guys she'll attract by wearing them are the ones she doesn't want. Tell her how inappropriate it is and how wearing them is beneath her. Heck, tell her anything you want, she won't listen anyway. The truth is, unless you forbid her or instigate a dress code at her school, she's going to dress how she wants (or more to the point, how all the other girls dress). Didn't you when your mom told you not to go out wearing spandex pants and that *Flashdance* off-the-shoulder sweater?

"Adults always think it's the boys trying to get sex,

but now it's mostly the girls."

—Jess, 13

Face it. Girls want to be popular with the boys and this is their way of doing it. They want to be in a relationship. Any kind of relationship. And here are the four different categories they have to choose from:

1. *Exclusive.* Sex within a committed relationship. Yeah, those are still legal in TeenTown, but rare.
2. *Hooking Up.* Physical contact without commitment. The modern-day "one nighter" which could range from kissing to group sex or anything in between. (Anything.)
3. *Friends.* Two people who have not investigated a sexual connection. Yet.
4. *Friends with Benefits.* They've done it, and at some point they'll do it again. They remain "unattached" and therefore available for an "exclusive" (with someone else) or hooking up (with someone else) without the threat of any "drama." This practice is popular with both boys and girls.

How can you tell which your teen is involved in? Good question, which of course means "there is no good answer." Because of course one leads into another and back again. You could start by listening, and keeping your ears open for the following codes:

- "Hanging out" = potential sex
- "Watching a DVD" = potential sex
- "Chillin'" = potential sex
- "Talking" = potential sex
- "We're not doing anything" = planning sex

Your Options:

- Discuss with your teens that it is often easy to feel pressured to engage in sexual behavior you may not be ready for. (And they might not be ready for it either.)
- Remind them that they are in charge of their body and what they do with it.
- Tell them the decisions they make tonight when you're not watching could have long-lasting physical, social, and emotional consequences.
- Make sure they know that regardless of what they choose, unprotected sex is never, ever okay.
- When all else fails, lock 'em up and throw away the key.

Coed Sleepovers

Coed sleepovers are nothing new. Except back in the day, they used to be called "marriage." As you may have noticed, times have changed. Once upon a time, if a teenage girl wanted to sleep at the home of two guys, she would be escorted to the nearest nunnery without passing Go or collecting $200. But nowadays a good nunnery is hard to find, and conversations such as this one are happening everywhere, every day . . .

Teen (girl): Mom, can I spend the night at Mike and Robby's?

Mom: I'm sorry, I thought I heard you ask—

Teen: A whole bunch of us are going to a movie and by the time it gets out it'll be too late for them to drive me all the way home.

Mom: Fine, I'll come get you.

Teen: No, you have to work early. I'm trying to be considerate.

Mom: So you're volunteering to sleep at two boys' apartment as a favor to me.

Teen: Yes. No. Sorta.

Mom: I'm sorry, but that's not going to happen.

Teen: Why not? Don't you trust me?

Mom: Yes. No. Sorta.

Teen: Mom!

Mom: You are sixteen years old.

Teen: You know Mike and Robby. They're just friends.

Mom: You are sixteen years old.

Teen: Have I ever done anything wrong?

Mom: No.

Teen: Then why can't I go?

Mom: You are sixteen years old.

Teen: What do you think is gonna happen?

Mom: Nothing.

Teen: Right!

Mom: Because you're not going.

Teen: Mom!

Mom: You are sixteen years old.

Teen: What did I do wrong?

Mom: Nothing. You are sixteen years old.

This conversation went on another two hours, pretty much repeating itself over and over and over until it ended in tears (from both), door slams (from the teen), and the consumption of an entire pint of Ben & Jerry's Chunky Monkey (for the mom). But you get the point. The truth is this girl had never been in any trouble—and her mother was determined to make sure she stayed that way.

No one knows who invented coed sleepovers, but maybe it was . . . mmmmm . . . Satan?

The concept of coed sleepovers is not worth debating. Which part of taking hormone-driven teenagers, turning off the lights, and leaving them unsupervised for eight hours behind a closed door seems like a good idea? The best that can happen is that nothing will happen. Tough to consider that a situation with a lot of upside. And if something does happen—and of course we're talking sex, folks—who would really be to blame? The teenagers? C'mon. That would be like blaming a dog for eating a steak left unattended on the kitchen table. The parents are the ones with the experience and knowledge and responsibility here. So it's a cop-out for the parent to say, "I trusted you and you burned me." That's not parenting, it's the opposite. It's an abdication of parenting. Parenting in this case is really simple:

"No."

The conversation is enlightening because it is a totally honest dialogue in which zero communication takes place. What did the teen learn? That's she's sixteen years old. She may have known that already. What did the mom learn? That an entire pint of Chunky Monkey is too much for one sitting.

No one did anything "wrong" in the talk. The fact is, there are thousands and thousands of words in the dictionary, yet none of them could have made the teen say "Oh, I get it now Mom, I can see it was a bad idea" or persuaded the mother to say "Well when you explain it that way, it's fine if you go." It was a perfect example of Human vs. TeenSpeak and no good could ever come of it. The interaction was fated for door-slamming and Chunky Monkey from the get-go.

The teen feels mistrusted. In her heart, she "knows" nothing will happen. Therefore, from her perspective, her mother is being unreasonable, and in the process making her look bad—like a little kid, being told what to do by her "mommy"—to her peers.

The mother does in fact trust her daughter. But she doesn't trust her lack of experience, and she doesn't trust the boys (what with them being boys and all).

Ultimately the mother did—and said—the right thing, which you should try when and if your teen brings up the topic of coed sleepovers (or any of the other million stupid things they'll want to do): "I love you and it's my job as your parent to do what I think is best for you. Even if you disagree and get angry with me about it." She also told her daughter that when she turns eighteen, she can stay out all night if she wants to.

True or not, she bought herself two years of peace with that one!

Homosexuality: A Tricky Teenage Time Just Got Trickier

As you knew before you even opened this book, raising teenagers is not for the faint of heart. (Or the faint of patience. Or the faint of wallet.) But raising a teenager with special needs, in this case societal judgment, will make your job that much trickier. Isn't that special indeed!?

"Gay" feelings can be a normal part of human development, and some experimentation is to be expected as teens grow into their sexual selves. Many times these feelings will be a short phase, but for other teens, finding love with a same-sex partner is their life's destiny. Many kids report feeling "different" since early on in their childhoods, only to later realize that they are gay. With so many other things going on in their lives and bodies, how is a teenager supposed to come to grips with mixed feelings about their sexual identity? Adolescents are confused enough trying to figure out what to order at the drive-thru! If your teen realizes that they really are gay, based upon how safe they feel they will tell you somewhere between that moment and never.

The good news is, even though the stigma of homosexuality still exists (in some places and families more than others), society has evolved to a place where being gay is becoming accepted if not yet fully embraced. Many states now have same-sex marriages and legal domestic partnerships on their books. Gay couples are routinely having children. Soon there will be messy gay divorces and ugly gay custody battles. Why should heterosexual families get to have all the fun?

These days teenagers have the freedom to "come out" early with their homosexuality and some will have no hesitation at all crashing through the proverbial closet door and announcing or even demonstrating their preference for a same-sex partner. Your teen may even choose to couple up openly with a partner at school, attend gay and lesbian support groups, and dance at the prom with his/her significant other. As parents, you may be surprised and even a bit uncomfortable by your teen's homosexuality, but in fact, if you have a teenager that is able to come out to the world comfortably and securely, these are kids that have high enough self-esteem to be themselves.

Is Your Teenager Gay?

Okay, so how do you know this might be a possibility? It's not uncommon for teens to be shy with (if not outright scared of) the opposite sex, so a disinterest in socializing with the opposite sex doesn't mean anything. Don't expect this to be obvious, like having them say "Hey folks, it's going to be a beautiful weekend, what do you say we take in that gay pride parade?" They probably won't prance around in drag looking like Cher, enter an Elton John look-alike contest, or become dedicated to TiVo'ing every episode of *The Ellen DeGeneres Show*. Instead the clues will likely be more subtle, such as "over-the-top" feelings for a same-sex friend. Most teens who are coming to grips with homosexual feelings will appreciate quiet parental support. "How was your day, please pass the carrots, and oh, are you gay?" may or may not fall into that category.

If as a parent you find yourself struggling with the issue of your child as being homosexual and you need support, there are groups that can provide help for you. PFLAG (Parents, Families, and Friends of Lesbians and Gays) is easily accessible via the web (*www.pflag.org*) and is one of the best. The truth is, if your teen is indeed gay, he or she will most likely struggle more with this than you do. Remember there is never an okay time or place to threaten, punish, or make harsh statements or judgments about your child for being homosexual. Doing so would be a huge parental mistake that you can never take back. Also, if you have other children in your home, encourage them to support their brother or sister.

Instead, be proud that your teenager is brave enough to walk their own path. Gays and lesbians are becoming more and more a mainstreamed fabric of society who grow up to be doctors and lawyers, teachers and actors, football players and NASA engineers. They have friends, lovers, life partners, and families who adore them. Gays and lesbians can also be wonderful mommies and daddies, especially if they've grown up with a good role model. (That would be you.)

So, if your teenager wants to go to the gay pride parade, take them. Wave a rainbow flag, wear your leather pants, pierce your nipples, and enjoy! (Well okay, you don't have to do the piercing the nipples part.)

CHAPTER 8

special k and other drugs: it's not just for breakfast anymore

Is there anything on God's Green Earth more upsetting to parents than drugs and alcohol? Other than not being able to work the remote, of course. But that aside, this is The One, and as The One it's worthy of being capitalized.

The reason why this is The One, of course, is that there are many different things happening at once. Think of it as a series of scary teenage planets aligning in just the wrong way: adolescents will experiment . . . peer pressure . . . looking to escape . . . rebellion. Now add the effects of the drugs themselves (and yes of course alcohol is a drug) and even at low levels (they will have little tolerance) their already questionable judgments become downright nonexistent. And finally, because your teens are likely partaking of their partying outside your home, that means they have to get back home somehow. And since you're the last person in the world they want to face in that situation, they will likely either be driving themselves while under the influence, or catch a ride with of their friends (also under the influence). The very thought is enough to drive parents to drink. Is it any wonder that parents get most of their gray hairs during their kids' teen years?

Parents understand one fundamental thing about this topic: when teens are impaired, they are risking their safety. And the worst part is, they don't even realize it. This exacerbates the danger factor even more. Protecting teens is tough enough—protecting them from themselves is even tougher.

And if this topic didn't already contain more wrinkles than a shuffleboard tournament in Miami Beach, here's one more: maybe you and/or your spouse are/were no strangers to indulging yourselves. So what do you cop to, and what do you lie about? Good question! Let's go see if we can find some good answers.

Recreational Drugs

Ah, recreation! The very word conjures up images of fun. But of course, one person's "fun" is another's "descent into madness," and in this case, the "fun" part is all theirs and the "descent into madness" part is all yours. Maybe now you know why the book is called *Teenagers Suck*.

Of course parents would prefer their teens have their fun in a "G-rated" sort of way. Didn't it look like Frankie Avalon and Annette Funicello were having fun in those movies when they all did The Twist on the beach? No one got high and no one got hurt (although the surfing was really fake looking). But let's face it, life is not "G-rated" anymore, and that's both your kids' loss and your problem.

"Yeah, I get high. All my friends get high.
Our parents drink. We smoke. What's the difference?"

—Riley, 16

"Recreational drugs" can be defined as any drug that's used with the specific intent of altering the mind (AKA "getting high," "catching a buzz," becoming "faded," "ripped," etc.). This pretty much includes all nonprescription drugs. But even prescription drugs fall into this category if a) the prescription belongs to someone else, or b) the legitimate recipient of the prescription is deliberately overusing (abusing) the drugs.

One of the great parental challenges in this area is going to be your own personal policy of self-disclosure. Odds are if you drink, your kids know it. Odds are if you use drugs, they don't. But realize that as you try to talk your teens out of drug/alcohol use/abuse, at some point they will ask if you ever used. Be ready with a good answer. But a "good answer" may not be what you think it is. If you have never used drugs, be honest and say so and tell them why you didn't. But if you have, denial may not work for you. That's because teens *love* to go to the "my parents don't understand" place, which (in their mind) gives them carte blanche to do whatever they want. Best to cop to "normal teen experimentation" which led you to realize that "drugs are bad." But don't admit to anything more, or else you'll go to the opposite end of the parental spectrum, which is the "they did it and turned out fine, so why can't I?" place. Don't feel badly about lying to your kids here. This one legitimately falls into the "it's for their own good" category. You made it through the whole Tooth Fairy thing, you can handle this one too.

Drug Distinctions

In terms of popularity, recreational drugs can be broken down into the following categories:

1. Alcohol
2. Nicotine (cigarettes)
3. THC (primarily marijuana)
4. Hallucinogens (PCP, LSD, mescaline, mushrooms, Ketamine, and Ecstasy)
5. Stimulants (cocaine being the most prevalent, amphetamine)
6. Opiates (heroin, Demerol, codeine)
7. Misused prescription drugs (including painkillers, barbituates, stimulants, and Rophypnol, also known as the date rape drug)
8. Inhalants (hairspray, deodorant, spray paint, canned whipping cream, paint thinner, gasoline, fabric spray and dry cleaning products, glue, felt-tip pens, spray cleaners for computers and cars, etc.)
9. Diet pills

While all of these can be harmful in excess, society doesn't treat them all equally. Alcohol and cigarettes are legal but (in theory) age-controlled, although due to massive anti-smoking efforts cigarettes have in many ways become déclassé (or, in TeenSpeak, "wack"). Diet pills can be used properly when paired with a healthy diet, but many teenage girls use them to fuel their starvation diets. Marijuana's status has become more complicated over the years, and while technically illegal, in many areas it has effectively become "decriminalized" for personal use.

Much scarier than the abuse of any of the above is the use of "harder" drugs. The bad news here is that there are a lot of these, the most popular of which are currently methamphetamine and Ecstasy, also known as "E" or "X" (the drug of choice at raves). This scary and long list of drugs that can do a lot of damage to the user (even the first time someone tries the drugs) includes cocaine (high end), glue (low end), and everything in between including LSD, barbituates, amyl nitrate, and Ketamine (AKA Special K), huffing inhalants, and abuse of prescription drugs such as Adderall and Ritalin.

Your best bet is to be aware of your teen's behavior. If there are any drastic changes in your teen's interests, eating or sleeping habits, or group of friends, consider drug use as a possible reason. Of course, if you come across any pills that don't look like aspirin or Midol, or any other suspicious-looking substances in your teen's possession, stop everything and confront them. What are these, where did you get them, and what are they for?

The "Other" Talk

Start with a short-but-sweet seemingly impromptu (no big family sit-down) conversation about drugs in general. Most schools now offer police-led D.A.R.E. (Drug Abuse Resistance Education) programs, so your kids already know what drugs are. Just ask them if they had the class. They'll say yes. Then ask them if they know drugs are bad for them. They'll say yes. Say "Good. I always knew you were smart." And leave it there, just like that. Your intended thought has been planted. Think of yourself as a modern-day Johnny/Joanie Appleseed.

If your teen comes home obviously stoned, that is not the time to get into a heavy conversation with them. (Remember, they're stoned! They'll just frustrate you by saying "Wow, man" a lot.) Save that for the next day . . . now that's a big family sit-down. If you happen to find marijuana in your teen's room, when snooping or otherwise, try instant confrontation. "What's this?" will get the ball rolling nicely. If they try the "I'm just holding it for a friend" tale, ask "Who, the Easter Bunny?" And don't be surprised if the ensuing conversation gets emotional, because odds are your teen may be holding on to some guilt for doing something he knows he shouldn't be doing. Culminate in watching your teen flush the pot down the toilet, and rest assured that with what that stuff costs nowadays, their tears will be real.

Drug Problems

Okay, "stoner" jokes may be amusing, but real drug addiction is anything but funny. For parents and families coping with a teen with drug problems, their world feels hopeless, frightening, and devastating. While this will hopefully never impact your family, realize that drug addiction is a serious problem (and unfortunately not uncommon) in today's world, and it's not always recognizable from the beginning. It's unlikely your fourteen-year-old is going to come in from basketball practice one day with needle track marks on his arm and say, "Hey Dad, check this out. Chip and I were mainlining some vicious tar today."

A clue that your young teenager may have a problem is that teens who develop drug addiction issues often begin experimenting significantly earlier than their peers. They may try alcohol from your liquor cabinet, take a hit off someone else's joint, swipe a couple of prescription painkillers, or try "huffing" (inhaling chemicals from aerosol products). These teenagers like the quickie high they feel and eventually, they go looking for much greater highs. But, younger teens are not as careful to cover their tracks (pun intended) and if you remain aware of missing or misused simple household medications and products, you will be able to interrupt this cycle and remove or lock up tempting items and get your teenager professional help.

As teenagers get older, their drug use broadens beyond gateway drugs like alcohol and marijuana, and while those substances can certainly be addictive, many use them occasionally and suffer no real damage. However, as a caution to parents, if you have addiction in your family tree, studies have shown that there is a genetic tie-in for addiction and your teenager is at even greater risk. If you do have addiction in your family, be straight with your teen and discuss it with them. If someone's addiction has led to a family tragedy, this is the time to tell them. Let them know that if they use, they will be putting themselves at a higher risk to develop serious problems. And that you love them and don't want them to get hurt.

Signs of Drug Use and Abuse

What are some signs of drug use/abuse? Behavioral changes are often the earliest and biggest clue. Watch your teenager for things like suddenly different sleeping/eating habits, a loss of interest in school or other activities previously enjoyed. You may also see your teenager abandoning old friends and hanging with a totally different peer group. Unexplained absences from the home and a total disconnect from family and friends who care are big warning signs.

Also, be on the lookout for excessive hostility, secrecy, lying, stealing, and cutting classes.

A Closer Look at Drug Addiction

James started drinking and smoking pot at the age of twelve, by age fourteen he had tried virtually everything to get high, and by the time he was sixteen he was hooked on methamphetamine. If he was at home, he slept. He no longer ate family meals, he disappeared at all hours of the day and night, he lost weight, his grades plummeted, he quit the soccer team, and it turned out that he was regularly stealing money from his parent's ATM accounts to pay for his habit. His parents noticed the changes in their son, but chalked it up to "just being a moody teenager." And sadly, by the time his parents took action, he was a full-blown meth addict. At sixteen, however, they had the legal power to place their son in a long-term rehabilitation program against his will. If they had waited much longer, James may never have gotten the help he needed, since once a teenager turns eighteen parents no longer have the ability to act as guardians.

The message we can take from James's story is that parents need to be vigilant about the signs of drug use, even the ones that seem to be easily explained away as "teenage moodiness." Parents should not ignore, deny, or excuse away any symptoms, even if they have no hard evidence—yet. Snoop through his car, her backpack, his room. If your child is abusing drugs, she is going to get sloppy about hiding it. If parents choose to look for proof, it is often right under their nose. Remember it is in your child's best interest to have parents willing to be concerned, confrontational, and if need be, have their teen committed for treatment. Better to be wrong too early, than right too late.

Dealing with Drinking

We don't know how it happens, but it does. Weeds some-how grow up through concrete, O. J. Simpson somehow finds new girlfriends, and teenagers somehow get alcohol. If you think about it, drinking really isn't the problem. It's when the drinking stops and the drunkenness begins that the problems start.

The average kid takes his or her first drink at age eleven. So hopefully, you've had the conversation about the dangers of drinking (and all its related stupidities, such as drunk driving) and locked up your alcohol before your child is a teenager. However, there's no denying that drinking becomes a much bigger factor in most kids' lives during their teen years.

As "normal" as teen drinking may be, it's vital that you don't stick your head in the sand here. It won't help your teen, and while you're spitting out sand you will realize the hard way why there's no such thing as the "Wolfgang Puck Sand Cookbook."

One step you can take is to try to limit their access to alcohol. If you have alcohol in your home, lock it up. No, putting it on a high shelf is not good enough. Lock it. With like a lock and stuff. If you keep beer or wine coolers in your fridge, keep tabs on how many and keep the running number on a Post-it or index card in the fridge, thus telling your teen you know exactly how many had better be there.

Your Baby Hits the Bottle

As it relates to teens, drinking is no different than any-thing else—different teens do it for different reasons, and with different results. Some may drink as a way to gain social status, AKA showing off. *See how much I can drink?* Others, perhaps on the shier/quieter side, may drink to remove inhibitions. The problem is, we have inhibitions for a reason. And when we lose them, it's like losing our car keys. Times ten.

Further, alcohol affects teen girls and guys differently, At the risk of generalizing gender differences, alcohol abuse often jump-starts testosterone levels in males, triggering aggressive behaviors such as fighting, foolhardy stunts, or "macho" behavior toward girls. This is a dangerous mix, because the effects of alcohol often have the opposite impact on females: inertia sets in and they often become placid. With both parties under the influence, and inhibitions removed, clothing can soon follow . . . leading to inappropriate sexual contact. Even though alcohol is the oldest and most commonly used "date rape" drug, there are others, such as GHB, which are administered through alcoholic and nonalcoholic drinks alike. Make sure your daughters know never to accept a drink from someone they don't trust, never to leave their drink unattended, and never to drink from a punch bowl.

When they first try drinking, teens will be totally unprepared for the effects of alcohol. With no built-up resistance, many will become totally plastered on one or two drinks. Of course, because of the delayed reaction alcohol has, they won't realize they're drunk until they have had three or four drinks, and by then their inhibitions are very relaxed.

Drinking and Driving

While happily not every rendezvous with a couple of beers at a party ends up in a Movie of the Week drama, nothing good can happen when drinking meets driving. The enemy here is the loss of judgment, AKA "I'm fine to drive." Whether this is your teen or a friend talking doesn't actually matter. You don't want your teen in a car with a driver who's been drinking, regardless of who it is. Your best bet to avoid this nightmare is total amnesty. Tell your teen (ahead of time!) that under no circumstances should they be in a car with a drinking driver (even if it's them), and if that happens they should call you and you will go pick them up. Anytime, anywhere, zero punishment. Zero. Because teens only need to be told things, oh, about six billion times, feel free to remind them of this policy each and every time they go out. Eventually they will beat you to it, at which point you will know they have heard you.

The Morning-After Talk

When your teen eventually comes home drunk (and it will happen), don't make a federal case out of it. Try to find out how much they drank (to be sure they don't have alcohol poisoning) and help them get to bed. The next day, wake them up early so they can deal with this conversation in all their hungover glory. But again go easy . . . the lesson they are learning in their throbbing heads is greater than any lecture you can lay on them at this point. If they are physically able without barfing everywhere, make them get up and fulfill their usual responsibilities. Between that and voicing your disappointment in their choices, they should learn a bit of a lesson. That's the most you can hope for here. And if they do barf, make them clean it up.

Putting Out the Fire and Curbing Cigarettes

Cigarettes suck. (Hmmm. Another book?) Most people who try them, which is just about everyone, come to this conclusion sooner rather than later. But some don't.

"When school, or work, or my family

stresses me out, smoking calms me down."

—Ashley, 18

Back in The Day (back before the phrase "Back in The Day" existed), teenage smokers were seen as "hoodlums" (a bad thing) to parents, but "outlaws" (a good thing) to other teens. Of course, that was then and this is now, and what we know now is that smoking is a killer epidemic that has single-handedly overwhelmed our health care system and caused cancers of all types to spike. Back then it was just thought of as something to do to relax. Incredibly, OB-GYNs often suggested smoking to their pregnant patients as a way to calm them down!

Because of the addictive nature of nicotine, cigarette companies figured out quickly that the sooner they could get a customer "hooked," the more years they would be able to buy cigarettes . . . before the product actually killed them. So they appealed to the concept that smoking was "hip," reeled in teens and young adults, and voilà, a generation of addicts was born. Interestingly, many years later that concept has come full circle. Now organizations like *www.thetruth.com* are based upon the idea that it's hip NOT to smoke. And it seems to be working. Perhaps that's what they call fighting fire with fire.

Still, teen smoking offers a unique challenge for parents. Keep in mind that unlike drinking, or sex, or trust issues, all of which are much more likely behavioral in cause and resolution, nicotine is so physically addictive that once your teen smokes, getting them to quit may be a much bigger chore than you think. But you do have one big thing going for you: research shows that general parental involvement in their childrens' lives is the number one way to prevent them from taking up smoking in the first place. Bruce Simons-Morton, PhD, of the NICHD (National Institute of Childhood Health and Development) Division of Epidemiology, Statistics and Prevention Research, surveyed over 1,000 middle-school students and asked children about their parents' involvement in their lives, and whether their parents checked to see if their children had done what they'd been asked to do. The results were clear: teens were less likely to smoke if their parents were more involved than if their parents were less involved. (Surprisingly, parents' expectations about smoking and whether an adult at home smoked did not significantly impact teens' decision to start smoking.) So make your argument early and often. Remind them (until you're sick of your own voice because hey, there's that not listening thing again) over and over how addictive and harmful cigarettes are. Hopefully, this will prevent any undue pain from smoking (except, of course, the pain of repeating yourself over and over and over . . .).

But okay, let's say you're too late for that. Your teen smokes, now what? Resist the temptation to slap the cigarette right out of his mouth. You might miss and loosen a tooth, and you already paid for braces. And don't make him eat them, a moment's satisfaction could create tremendous gastrointestinal distress and/or expensive shrink bills later and you'd be paying for those too. If it's a recent experiment, appealing to her teen vanity might not be a bad place to start, especially if you have girls. The premature aging of smoking to the skin, hair, and nails is very real. Smokers' teeth yellow like a hamster's. Toss in there the concepts that cigarettes are expensive, will totally ruin their lung capacity for sports, and that a smoker's cough is not hot. Close by pointing out someone you know who died due to smoking. (And you surely know someone.) If this still doesn't do it, your best bet is to ban smoking inside the house (it stinks!), make your teen wash their own clothes regularly (they stink!), be sure the smoke detectors in your house work (just in case), and take your teen to your family doctor for treatment. Remember that smoking is not a habit. Eating popcorn with cheese on it every night in front of the TV is a habit. Saying "you know?" is a habit. Tying your right shoe before your left every single time is a habit. Smoking is an addiction. Get help and get it fast. The longer your teen smokes, the more damage done and the tougher to get them to quit. And the longer they smoke, the longer you suffer. A lose-lose.

To review: smoking is disgusting, expensive, and unhealthy. In a teen's eyes, what's not to like?

10 Songs Not about Parenting Teenagers
(But Could Have Been)

1. "Breakdown Dead Ahead," Boz Scaggs
2. "Bridge Over Troubled Water," Simon & Garfunkel
3. "Crazy Train," Ozzy Osbourne
4. "Don't Be Cruel," Elvis Presley
5. "Drinking Bout You," Big & Rich
6. "Highway to Hell," AC/DC
7. "Hold On Loosely (But Don't Let Go)," .38 Special
8. "My Way," Frank Sinatra
9. "Reelin' In the Years," Steely Dan
10. "Runaway," Del Shannon

CHAPTER 9

rebel yell

And now here it is, the final chapter. Both of this book and in your story of rearing your kids. You have raised your older teens the best you could. Now it's just about time to release the hounds into the big, bad world. Are they ready? Hell no! The bigger question is, are you? And the answer is . . . Hell no! Your work is not done, and never will be. They won't be kids forever, but they will be your kids forever. Nothing wrong with that. Okay, all seriousness aside . . .

"Paying your dues." It's not a particularly humorous phrase, especially when compared to such classics as "Up your nose with a rubber hose" or "They're one sandwich short of a picnic." And yet, there is something funny about how "paying your dues" works. People always make it sound like a temporary situation. People lie! You never stop paying your dues! You'd think whoever is collecting all these dues would own an island off Spain by now and be satisfied, but no!

Remember way back when you were in eighth grade, you "owned" middle school. You were the "big" kids. The very next year, as a high school freshman, you were back at the bottom of the ladder again! Gradually you moved up, gaining confidence and experience and privileges and status. Finally you were a senior, and you "owned" high school. Then you graduated—parties, congratulations—you were at the top of the world, ma! The world was your oyster—for one short summer. Until you were a college freshmen! You graduated all right—right back to the bottom! Eventually your college days ended. And then . . . you got it. Back to the bottom again out in the real world. Time to "pay your dues." Temporarily, of course. (Wink wink!)

But let's not get ahead of ourselves. There is a little time left before the birdies leave the nest and follow your path to adulthood, so how best to spend it? What's the endgame? (Glad you asked!)

The Beginning of the End . . . or the End of the Beginning

Remember how your now-teen showed up in your life gradually? Nine months in utero, then another couple of years before they could walk and talk and learn how to break stuff and throw your life into total disarray? Well things are coming full circle now, and as everyone knows if you go around in circles long enough you will eventually get dizzy, fall over, and perhaps even barf. Something to look forward to. But anyway, the point (and yes there is a point) is that just as they arrived gradually, so too will they leave gradually. Or at the very least, sporadically, which is actually gradually's second-cousin-once-removed.

As your teen leaves adolescence, they will be leaving other things as well. You, for example. They will either be physically moving on (to college or to their own place) or emotionally moving on (making more and more of their own decisions). Probably both. When you think about this, what's the first thing that comes to mind? Acapulco? Okay, what's the second thing that comes to mind? Right—that having your teen move away from you in either a literal or figurative sense is a bad thing. This is not true. It is a good thing, for both of you. (See: Vacation, Acapulco.)

As simple as this may seem, this is actually the first—and biggest—step in letting go: for you to realize that it's actually best for everybody. Up until now you have probably believed that the more involvement you had in your child's (and later teen's) life, the better off both of you were. And you were right—right up until now, that is. Hanging on now would embody "diminishing returns." You know, like how a little cosmetic surgery makes people look better, but too much makes them look like Michael Jackson? The truth is, the more of yourself you have invested in your child over these years, the tougher this will be to accept. (And if you happen to like the way Michael Jackson looks, it will be totally impossible for you to accept.) You must be wondering, how could less of you possibly equal something positive for them? Hmmm. Well let's take a walk down Memory Lane . . .

Flashback
Your Parents' House, circa a long time ago

It's the day after your eighteenth birthday. You are wearing one of your birthday gifts. You love it. You have fun plans with your friends. One of your parents enters. You know which one.

Your Parent: You're all dressed up!

18-Year-Old You: Everybody's going shopping and I'm going to spend some birthday money and then we're all going out to dinner after.

Your Parent: Oh.

18-Year-Old You: (this is not good) Oh?

Your Parent: (the "guilt" voice) Never mind.

18-Year-Old You: (this is definitely not good) No, what?

Your Parent: It's just that I just thought maybe we could spend some quality time together. Watch reruns on TV or play "Old Maid." I planted an azalea; maybe we could just sit in silence all evening and watch it grow?

18-Year-Old You: (I'm in hell) Oh.

Your Parent: I mean, it won't be long until you're out in the world, and then I'll be here all by myse—but never mind, you go ahead and have fun, I need to reorganize the spice rack anyway.

18-Year-Old You: (I will never, ever do this to my kids, ever) No! I mean . . . I love organizing the spice rack!

Your Parent: Really?! It is fun, isn't it!

18-Year-Old You: (um, no!) Sure is! So I'll just change out of my new clothes and into my grubbies and call all my friends and cancel on them at the last minute so I can stay home and do nothing instead.

Your Parent: Great! We'll make Pop Tarts!

18-Year-Old You: (No matter how many gray hairs they give me, or how much weight I gain due to stress eating, or how many wet towels I have to pick up off their floor, I will never, ever do this to my kids, never) Yum!

You're not a bad person. You're a parent. There's a difference. You gave them life. So maybe now let them live it?

"The day we dropped Kelli off at college I thought, raising her wasn't easy. She was a tough kid and an even tougher teenager. And now that she's grown into this beautiful, smart, independent young woman, our reward is that she leaves us? Where did we go wrong?"

—Jonathan, Kelli's Father

". . . And at the same time I thought, wow, look at that beautiful, smart, independent young woman. Where did we go right?"

—Holly, Kelli's Mother

Giving Up (Some) Control: A Modern Day Fable

Once upon a time in Parentland there lived a single mother named D. J. (Her initials have been changed to protect the innocent.) D. J. raised her daughter Claire completely alone. D. J. worked two jobs (three for a while), and was a loving, hands-on mom who selflessly sacrificed her own personal life (read, didn't get any for years) to make Claire's life everything it could possibly be and then some. Claire, meanwhile, flourished in the one-on-one attention and became one of those non-weird kids with a 4.0 grade point average you read about but somehow never give birth to. And she was even one of those nice 4.0 kids!

Between her junior and senior years, Claire was asked to join some friends on a summer trip. Claire was excited. Although she had been well-loved at home, she had also been overprotected. Although Claire was seventeen and she had never been away from D. J. for more than a sleepover, D. J. knew and approved of the friends who would be involved, so that wasn't an issue. The trip was well planned and would be thoroughly chaperoned so those weren't issues either. All systems were go. All D. J. had to do was sign off on it. At which point D. J. handled it the way most parents would handle it.

She totally freaked out.

Faster than you could say "My baby is leaving me!" D. J. had a dozen reasons why this whole idea was completely unacceptable. Ludicrous, even. These included "You need to have a summer job!" and "You're too young to be out of my sight for two weeks!" and "You can't remember to throw cans into the recycling, how are you going to take care of yourself for that long?" She might have even added "You have a goldfish to feed!" for good measure. But later, after the eyes had been rolled and the tears had been cried and the doors had been slammed, D. J. finally settled down with a cup of tea and realized what was really happening. This wasn't about Claire. This was about D. J.

On one hand, it was about "What is the responsible parenting move here?" That is what D. J. had lived by for these seventeen years and was her default parenting position. And on the other hand, it was a clear-cut case of PENS: Pre-Empty Nest Syndrome. And on the third hand, it was about—oh wait, there are only two hands, so let's just stick with those.

For all those years, D. J.'s life and Claire's life were virtually indistinguishable. D. J. literally had dedicated her life to her daughter, and in doing so had given up much of her own identity. She was "Claire's mom" first and D. J. second. So of course the idea of a separation—not just a physical separation but (even worse to D. J.) a philosophical separation—was crushing.

Acapulco vacations aside, the phrase "Empty Nest Syndrome" does not conjure up many "Whoo hoo!" images of a lot of parents wearing lampshades on their heads in some gigantic conga line. Instead it describes sadness. Longing. Separation. That's because parents and teens have quickly become two trains passing in the night. Theirs is steaming toward "Their Gain" and yours is barreling straight to "Your Loss."

As a result, it's no wonder Claire's trip seemed like a bad idea to D. J. From her point of view, it was a three strikes situation. Strike one: Claire would be out of her sight/control (and therefore in potential "danger" since no chaperone could ever take care of her like her own mother). Strike two: D. J. would miss Claire while she was away. And strike three: Claire actually *wanted* to go! To voluntarily be away from D. J.! Oh, there was some upside in this scenario—but it was all Claire's. And because so much of her own life was wrapped up in her daughter's, D. J. couldn't see Claire as a totally separate entity. So in effect, Claire's happiness was pretty darned unimportant to the one person who had dedicated her life to creating it. Ah, the irony.

And thus was the PENS created—that Pre-Empty Nest Syndrome. (Like Christmas shopping, no sense in waiting till the last minute.) D. J. had seen the future, and in the future Claire was happy and D. J. was nowhere in sight.

If this were a different kind of fable, it would be time to cue the big bad wolf or play out the porridge scene or have three little pigs show up and start running around. But it isn't. Instead we just had two people who were, at that moment, not speaking to one another. Who instead were in separate rooms (one on the kitchen phone, one text-messaging) telling their best friends how unreasonable the other was being.

Claire: omg i m so mad

D. J.: "I am so upset!"

Claire: I cant believe my mom can u

D. J.: "I can't believe Claire! She's in her room just crushed. It's going to take forever for her to get over this."

Claire: r u watching gossip gurl 2nite

D. J.: "I know her, she's going to obsess about this!"

Claire: omg henry from the tudorz is soooooo cute

D. J.: "Believe me, she won't eat, she won't sleep, she won't even think about anything but this summer trip."

Claire: i wish my name was chelsea or miranda or uma

D. J.: "I may have to get her into therapy so she can get past this and move on."

Claire: omg i hate my frecklez

D. J.: "Poor kid's in there beating herself up over this."

Claire: i so want pinkberry right now yum

D. J.: "I should go in and talk to her. I'm sure she's just sitting there waiting for me."

Claire: omg we should so get r hair cut short

D. J.: "I am not letting her go on this trip. Not, not, not!"

D. J. let Claire go on her trip eventually. And of course it was fine eventually. And they all lived happily ever after. Eventually.

Endgame: The Sky's the Limit

Imagine your teen's entire life as an airplane. Charles Lindbergh had "The Spirit of St. Louis." Call your teen's "The Spirit of [insert your teen's name here]." When [insert your teen's name here] was born, the plane took off, traveling through time and space as planes are wont to do. You were the pilot and he was simply a drooling baby-powdered passenger who just sat there waiting to be fed. As he grew into childhood, he started to get up once in a while to go to the bathroom and hit the "call" button and fall asleep during the movie.

When she got older, she started to take on some actual modest responsibilities. Metaphorically let's say she moved up to become a flight attendant. Yes, she made mistakes, but when she did it was really no worse than a dropped tray and trays can be picked up. As she made her way through adolescence and her individualism started to kick in and she began to make some of her own decisions, she joined you in the cockpit and you became co-pilots of her own life. You were still in charge, but she was learning and growing, and you found yourself comfortably sharing your knowledge and expertise with her on an entirely new level. You even let her take the controls once in a while, for a few minutes at a time, although you were sitting right there in the big chair just in case.

But that was then and this is, of course, now. And things are about to change. Actually they already *have* changed. Your copilot is starting to think about flying his own life. You can't possibly get your head around that, since when you look at your copilot you can remember taking him for his first haircut and spraying Bactine (remember that?) on his boo-boos and reading him bedtime stories. He's a little kid, right? And everybody knows a little kid can't possibly fly a plane.

And yet . . .

As you eye your co-pilot, you realize he is eyeing you right back. Only it's not exactly you he's eyeing—it's your seat. The pilot seat. And now for the first time you realize he has brought a parachute on board. You chuckle at this and ask, "Why do you need a parachute? Don't you trust my flying?" And he responds, "This is my plane. This parachute isn't for me. It's for you."

And then you want to cry.

"My mom starts to cry when she thinks about me moving out.

I say, don't worry Mom, I'll be back all the time

to do laundry and raid the fridge and borrow money.

That's when my mom stops crying. And my dad starts."

—Ian, 18

You realize your time in the cockpit is over and it's time for your child to fly her own plane. You hope you have taught her enough to avoid the storm clouds and weather the turbulence and battle the headwinds that lie ahead. So strap on that parachute, and if you still feel like crying, go ahead. You deserve it. You done good. But after the tears have dried, go ahead and book that trip to Acapulco. You deserve that too.

And now there's nothing left to say except . . .

Geronimo!

reference books to complement teenagers suck

For Chapter 1: Hormones: How the Simplest Creatures Become Criminally Insane

The Care & Keeping of You: The Body Book for Girls by Valorie Schaefer

What's Going on Down There? Answers to Questions Boys Find Hard to Ask by Karen Gravelle

For Chapter 2: Mars, Venus, & TeenTown, and Chapter 3: You're Not Leaving the House Looking Like That!

Real Issues, Real Teens: What Every Parent Needs to Know by T. Suzanne Eller

Are You Losing Control? The Common Sense Guide to Parenting Teens by Carolyn Bergmann

Yes, Your Teen Is Crazy! Loving Your Kid Without Losing Your Mind by Michael J. Bradley

For Chapter 4: What We Have Here Is a Failure to Communicate

You're Grounded: How to Stop Fighting and Make the Teenage Years Easier by Vanessa Van Petten

Generation MySpace by Candice Kelsey

Totally Wired: What Tweens and Teens Are Doing Online by Anastasia Goodstein

Promise Me You Won't Freak Out by Doris Fuller and Natalie Fuller

159

For Chapter 5: Papa's Got a Brand New Bag . . . of House Rules

The Teen Whisperer: How to Break Through the Silence and Secrecy of Teenage Life by Mike Linderman

A Parent's Guide: How to Reach Your Teen: Parenting Bootcamp by Jeff A. Parke

For Chapter 6: Relationships Between Drama Queens & Kings

Queen Bees and Wannabes: Helping Your Daughter Survive Cliques, Gossip, Boyfriends and Other Realities of Adolescence by Roselind Weiseman

Raising Cain: Protecting the Emotional Life of Boys by Dan Kindlon, PhD, and Michael Thompson, PhD

Reviving Ophelia: Saving the Selves of Adolescent Girls by Mary Pipher and Ruth Ross

For Chapter 7: Sex: From Hanging Out to Hooking Up!

How to Talk with Teens About Love, Relationships and S-E-X: A Guide for Parents by Amy G. Miron, MS, and Dr. Charles D. Miron, PhD

My Child Is Gay: How Parents React When They Hear the News by Bryce McDougall

The Real Truth About Teens & Sex: From Hooking Up to Friends with Benefits, What Teens Are Thinking, Doing and Talking About and How to Help Them Make Smart Choices by Sabrina Weill

100 Questions You'd Never Ask Your Parents by Nancy Armstrong and Elizabeth Henderson (Parents & Teens)

For Chapter 8: Special K and Other Drugs: It's Not Just for Breakfast Anymore

Choices & Consequences: What to Do When a Teenager Uses Alcohol and Drugs by Dick Schaefer

When to Worry: How to Know If Your Teen Needs Help and What to Do About It by Lisa Boesky, PhD

Drugs and Your Kid by Peter D. Rogers, PhD, and Lea Goldstein

For General Help:

Stop Negotiating with Your Teen: Strategies for Parenting Your Angry, Manipulative, Moody or Depressed Adolescent by Janet Sasson Edgette

7 Things Your Teenager Won't Tell You and How to Talk About Them Anyway by Jenifer Lippincott and Robin M. Deutsch

Teen-Proofing: Fostering Responsible Decision Making in Your Teenager by John Rosemond

Computer Spy Software:
- Webwatcher
- Parental Control Suite
- Sentry PC
- Ace Spy Software
- Net Nanny – For Younger, Less Savvy Teens
- Cybersitter – For Younger, Less Savvy Teens

index